The FIVE PILLARS to raise Your Child in Turbulent Times

The Secret to Bringing Up
Happy and Resilient Children

Dr. Orlando David Garcia

2022 © Orlando David Garcia

All rights reserved.

No part of this publication may be reproduced, stored in a retrieval system, or transmitted, in any form, by any means, electronic, mechanical, photocopying, recording or otherwise without the express written permission of the author.

About The Author

Dr. Orlando David Garcia is a Cuban Canadian medical doctor and a Neurologist who did research in the area of coma and brain death. In 1992 while working in the Institute of Neurology and Neurosurgery in Havana, Cuba, he was awarded a National Prize for the best scientific work of the year for a study on Heart Rate Variability in Coma and Brain Death. [a,b] He is happily married to Crystal, his wife of 25 years, and they have two children.

Dedication

To my wife Crystal, for applying the principles of this book in the upbringing of our children,

to our daughter Sarah Lidia and our son David Jeremiah, a gift from God to us,

to my parents, Orlando and Zaida who built their house with the five pillars, upon the rock,

to my sisters Iliana and Lidia for being examples of love, faith, and dedication to family while having outstanding professional careers,

to my relatives and friends.

For Whom Is This Book?

This book is for all mothers, fathers, grandparents, homeschoolers, teachers, educators, and young couples dreaming of having children in happy, resilient families.

Acknowledgments

I wish to thank my cousin Silvia Williams, a longtime outstanding educator and fine artist (painter), for her support as a reader and suggestions for word changes. Dr. Leonid Maximenkov, Ph.D., Pedagogue, and Historian, for his support as a reader and comments. My uncle Mauro García Triana, Ambassador and Historian, a pillar of our family, for his encouragement and reading of the book.

CONTENT

Introduction	11
LOVE	**15**
DISCIPLINE	**45**
FREEDOM	**67**
INSTRUCTION	**89**
WORLDVIEW	**121**
AFTERWORD	**155**
References	157

INTRODUCTION

We live in an age of swift transformation. Our World is shaped by convergent new knowledge and technologies, from Biotechnology to Robotics, Space Technology to Quantum Computing, Artificial Intelligence, and Virtual Reality. New weapons like nuclear bombs and hypersonic missiles pose an existential threat to humanity. Our biology remains stable, almost static, compared to the fast-paced developments in science and technology. In this panorama, signs, and symptoms of a social crisis abound in industrialized countries. A complex web of factors may contribute to mental illness. In industrialized nations populations in fact may be increasingly overfed, malnourished, sedentary, and sleep-deprived, as well as socially isolated.[1]

The average age of onset of mental disorders is 14.5 years—including anxiety and depression—according to a large-scale study in which researchers analyzed data from multiple sources.[2] This situation contrasts with many traditional cultures that lack depression entirely. Add to this our high rates of suicide and the global ubiquity of antidepressant drugs. Our materialistic culture is stripping us of our self-worth and destroying the very foundation of our happiness. When we have lost our vigor and joy, have to depend on external sources for our sense of worth, and are not happy in ourselves, we are vulnerable to depression and anxiety. Suicide is the second leading cause of death among youth and young adults (15-34 years) in Canada.[3] Youth and young adults ages 10–24 years account for 14% of all suicides in the United States, and suicide is the third leading cause of death for young people, accounting for 6,643 deaths.[4] For youth ages 10-14, suicide is the second leading cause of death.[4] In Canada and the United States, obesity rates have increased significantly during the last 30 years.[5] Childhood obesity is a public health issue for governments and families alike. In the United States, the prevalence of obesity among children and adolescents aged 2-19 years was around 20% in 2017-2020, putting about 14 million at risk for poor health.[6]

Psychological health and social well-being correlate negatively with individualism, materialism, hyper-competition, greed, and overwork.[7] Let's talk about isolation: In the U.S., about 40% of marriages now end in divorce and for the first time in American history, more than 50% of adults aren't married.[8] It's not just relationships though. One-quarter of households consist of people living alone.[8] In 2015, there were approximately 13.6 million single parents in the United States, and those parents are responsible for raising 22.4 million children.[9] This number represents 27% of children under 21 in the United States. We have a lot of possessions: now what? We tend to believe that more will make us happy than it actually does, and studies show positive effects only up to a certain income level. We have all been there: having to work more, becoming less happy, and making ourselves more stressed. There is an alternative—perhaps we can focus on living more simply, spending more time with family, friends, and nature—and providing for ourselves what we need from life instead of needless wants. The family, the traditional foundation of society, is undermined through policies, education, and cultural trends. Is this a good path? The answer is no. We have already seen it. A family crisis is a serious issue that touches the core of our society and our lives. Family is the bedrock of society, and it must be preserved and protected as one of the essential things in life! Our culture developed from pillars such as family, community, and tradition, and they are currently under attack like never before in our history. Hopefully, our families will be prepared to find covert and succeed while confronting the daring enterprise that seeks to erase millennia of culture.

The highest values, purpose, and meaning are daily bread for youths; starvation from this nourishment can put them in peril of anxiety, depression, demoralization, and existential crisis. We may be easily distracted by the myriad of problems and then lose track of perennial fundamental principles for the education of our children. What can parents, families, educators, and others do? This book will help you refocus; it delineates the essential pillars for a solid foundation for your child's education. If you want to raise your child to be happy and healthy, this book will help. Is your little one feeling sad? Worried? Scared? Or maybe angry? Your children need to develop a positive mindset to accomplish their greatest potential. This book will help you instill in your child all the proven indicators of positive mental health in children: affection, resilience, positivity, curiosity, persistence, and self-control![10] Focusing on time-tested intertwined principles reinforcing each other, your efforts as a parent, grandparent, educator, or homeschooler will fructify in flourishing lives and virtuous individuals. Your children will benefit from healthy, happy, and responsible lives, the prerequisite for an ethical society.

The book has five chapters, each dedicated to one of the pillars for a well-balanced, solid education of children, and an afterword as the conclusion. I have consulted more than two hundred and thirty sources, including many from the peer-reviewed medical literature.

LOVE

"Love is not affectionate feeling, but a steady wish for the loved person's ultimate good as far as it can be obtained." [11]
—C. S. Lewis

At the foundation of Western Civilization is the transforming ideal of love. In one of his letters, Saint Paul tells his disciple Timothy these words "for God has not given us a spirit of fear, but of power and of love and of a sound mind."[12] This verse has a deep religious meaning. But also—if we look closely, we will see three virtues represented in one sentence. They correspond to the ideal central to each one of the historical pillars of our civilization. For the Romans, the cardinal virtue was power and strength. For the Judeo-Christian mind, the highest value was love, whereas it was arguably moderation for the Greeks. Here we will look at the importance and power of *Love* for a child's education. *Discipline* points to the development of the virtue of moderation aiming at higher goals and aspirations. *Freedom* empowers as much as it helps unleash a child's potential as a unique human being to develop and flourish. Each one of these virtues is in itself learned and developed. They will also reinforce each other, creating a solid frame for fruitful *Instruction* for life. Finally, these virtues do not merge in a vacuum. They need a coherent, truth-based *Worldview* that glues them together. Then a child's identity and confidence will develop harmoniously. A well-balanced education will provide security and a sense of well-being to a child. The positive effect of such education will last well into adulthood.

The Meanings of Love

In his book *The Four Loves* from 1960, C. S. Lewis[13]—the Oxford Scholar and author of *Chronicles of Narnia*—explores the nature of love from a Christian and philosophical perspective. Starting from St. John's words "God is Love," the author initially contrasted "Need-love" (such as the love of a child for its mother) and "Gift-love" as supremely expressed in God's love for humanity. The natures of these primary forms of love are more complicated than they appear at first glance. A child's need for parental comfort is a necessity, not a selfish indulgence. On the other hand, out of appropriate balance, parental Gift-love can damage a child's development rather than being beneficial. As we will explore throughout this book, the larger context of love includes discipline, freedom for growth, instruction, and a consistent Worldview.

The best way to begin this chapter is by touching briefly on the various meanings behind this single four-letter word in English. The Greeks had a different word for what most of us call love. First, Agape[13] is unconditional love, wanting the good of the other, a reflection of God's love. Also known as charity, love exists regardless of changing circumstances. This selfless love is the greatest, a central virtue. Saint Paul most beautifully writes about it in his first letters to the Corinthians. Love is patient and kind. Love does not envy or boast; it is not proud or rude. Love does not insist on its own way; it is not irritable or resentful; it does not rejoice at wrong but rejoices in the right. Love bears all things, believes all things, hopes all things, endures all things. Love never fails.

Storge[13] is a form of empathy. It is the bond and liking of family members and other people who relate to us in familiar ways. One of the best examples is the love and affection of a parent for their child. Parental love is the most natural, affectionate, and widely present in society. This form of love is genuine, without coercion, and develops due to fondness due to familiarity. This form of affection does not spring from characteristics deemed worthy of love. Storge transcends most discriminating factors.

Philia[13] is the love between friends. The bond exists between people who share common interests and values, enjoy their company, or share activities—traditionally regarded as a form of love freely chosen. Some vulnerabilities and dangers are also implicit in friendships. In the words of C. S. Lewis: "to the Ancients, friendship seemed the happiest and most fully human of all loves; the crown of life and the school of virtue. The modern world, in comparison, ignores it". And, "Friendship is unnecessary, like philosophy, like art.... It has no survival value; rather it is one of those things which give value to survival."

Eros[13] is love in "being in love" or "loving" someone. Eros contrasts with raw sexuality; it is not that. Eros is like fire; when kept in the fireplace, it lights and warms the house, but it destroys it when out of its proper place. In all its splendor, Eros, like fire, can be neutral itself; it "may urge to evil as well as good." The modern tendency for Eros to become an idol to people when they fully submit themselves to its urge only increased in recent decades.

A Well-Balanced Foundation

Parents desire happiness, maturity, and fulfillment for their children. We dedicate time, effort, and mental and material resources to help them develop. We desire to see them succeed and achieve their goals.

Sometimes the stress and demands of modern life distract us from the most important thing our children need to thrive and flourish. What they need the most is love. A home is an important place in our lives. We are not better off separated from our loved ones. Unfortunately, school and daycare institutions cannot replace the role of the home as the provider of love. We live in a materialistic society, where love is frequently ignored or trivialized; current education centers on individual achievement, where accountability and measurement are standard requirements for any child's success. However, affection is intangible and cannot be subject to the same kind of evaluation. As an essential need, love is neglected in many ways, as if it were irrelevant. In a fast-changing technological culture, we prize skills and information. But we frequently ignore the power of true love. Is it wise to neglect a force capable of transforming the World and creating great civilizations? As parents, we need to harness it to help our children become healthy and responsible adults.

As parents, we risk putting too much pressure on our children to succeed. We may spend great energy and effort in making them competitive in school, sports, music, and other activities. However, we need to find a balance. The lack of parental love can be detrimental to all other areas of development. It can put our children under unnecessary stress. Lack of parental affection can affect health, mental and emotional development, and learning. Love from parental figures can alleviate the consequences of health and social problems. Love is the glue that ties together all other growth areas in the developing child. What your young children need most of all is that you gratify their hunger for contact and closeness. When the need for bonding is satisfied, the child can develop healthy tendencies to explore and learn through play and other age-related activities. In the absence of warmth, physical touch, and bonding, the biological trend toward a fear-fight-or-flight response will tend to inhibit healthy development. In such situations, the negative impact includes both the absence of love—with its plethora of benefits—plus the prevalence of a negative biological pattern of response that can hamper a child's development.

A balanced education provides long-lasting benefits. This investment in childhood tends to pay off with flourishing in adulthood. Unfortunately, parents' consistently negative behaviors can negatively impact long into adulthood. Studies show that adults who were harshly disciplined as children are more likely to suffer from mental problems like depression, anxiety, and addiction. It is important to mention that adults overprotected during childhood also struggle with anxiety and poor self-image. The lack of personal freedom prevents children from opportunities to develop coping skills. Here and throughout this book, I will emphasize the importance of balance. Love, Discipline, Freedom, Instruction, and a sound Worldview mutually reinforce each other. Focusing on this, parents can create a life-long solid foundation. Note that those key fundamentals are the same that adults need to flourish in life. This continuity, if not anything else, should reassure us about the wisdom of guiding our lives, and our children's lives, according to these time-tested principles.

Parental Love

Warmth, affection, and love are critically important in a child's life. Appreciation includes love in all forms—except for its meaning as Eros. In the rest of this book, love will be used in the former broad sense unless otherwise pointed out. Research into early child development has increased in the past several decades. We now have a deeper understanding of the rapid growth of the brain in the first four years of life. We can have a new appreciation of the need to harness the potential of plasticity during those critical first years. The importance of the brain and its plasticity in early life is increasingly appreciated. It is not an overstatement to say that the first four years after birth are critical for brain development. The human brain growth the most during this time, setting the foundation for learning. The daunting task of adapting to the World, learning a language, and social and emotional skills never stop impressing parents and researchers alike. Love is the early and primary gluing ingredient in the recipe for solid and lasting human responsibility and happiness.

Specific natural capacities have a solid biological foundation, but in this strength underlies a trap for parents. Affection appears as a built-in or "ready-made" capacity. We come to expect it without considering the need to develop it. Love needs cultivation; it involves both instruction and interactive parent-child behavior. Natural consequences will follow whether we ignore this dynamic or actively consider the best way to educate our children. For us parents, and ever pertinent reminder: the more we make love central in our own lives, the easier to share it. It becomes a mutually enriching endeavor as part of our children's education.

It is my firm belief that to educate effectively; we need love. One may think I can teach rules, knowledge, and skills without love. It is true, but love is indispensable for the integral development of a child. As adults, too, we need to grow in love continually. There is no robust and happy family without sharing of affection. Love brings enjoyment when we perform a task. Love is a source of strength and brings patience and understanding, essential in teaching. The empathetic nature of love allows us to see our child as a person subjected to struggles and challenges. When we instill in them the feeling that we care for them, we create a strong foundation. It becomes a powerful motivation for growth in all other areas.

Instructing the child is more than teaching skills. We should look at the person "as a whole" to help them flourish.

The language of love can be as rich as life itself. First, be intentional in the desire to grow in love. Cultivate love as a foundation of your lives as parents. Be always a role model of love for your child. When love is the foundation, it will expand into all different areas. They will love to play and practice sports, discover friendships, and the excitement of exploring the World. This way, you provide an environment conducive to cultivating the child's natural curiosity. Gradually they will develop their interests and become capable of moving into new spaces of freedom and responsibility. The family is the first community and a model for later life in society. A vibrant, loving family is a strong mini community; it is preparatory for adult life. When children can express themselves with authenticity, growth and transformation become an ongoing process. They are more likely to become a responsible, positive force in society. Then as grown-ups, they will become a living testimony of the love practiced at an early stage in their lives.

Nature Versus Nurture

First, a few words about a long-standing debate in biology: "nature versus nurture."[14] Nature is related to the idea of natural biological factors and is affected by genetics, inheritance, and other physical aspects. Nurture we associate with the environment, the result of experience, learning, and interacting with the World. The debate is about understanding two groups of factors shaping a person's development and future characteristics. The nature vs. nurture controversy has fascinated scientists and philosophers for centuries. Humans come into the world with an innate capacity for knowledge, contended Plato.[15] The source of this knowledge is primary from the reality of the "forms" to the soul. In Aristotle's view,[16] humans gain knowledge through experience and education. Throughout the centuries, thinkers and philosophers developed these two perspectives. The 21-century understanding is that nature and nurture are essential factors in shaping who we are. Geneticists agree that both nature and nurture influence human behavior. DNA is inherited but has a remarkable capacity: it responds to the environment.[17,18] Scientists now understand that while nature plays a part in how a child develops, the early environment powerfully shapes a child's potential for healthy physical, emotional, mental, and social growth. Genes are not set in stone—they can be turned "on" or "off." Our genes influence our behavior, and they are affected by the environment, and it is almost always a dynamic interaction of both. The complex interplay between nature and nurture happens at multiple levels: from the tiny cells to the person "as a whole" with all the complexity of human beings in their social environment.

For the benefit of our children, we need to understand that nature and nurture work together in a complementary fashion. Any child disability will require early detection and specialized care. The earlier the better to maximize learning potential and development. If a child is delayed in one area, this can affect development in other areas as well. Early intervention services are designed to help parents, caretakers and teachers understand their child's needs, and give them interventions that will allow the child to reach their full potential. At the same time, we should be prepared to educate children of exceptional talent first by recognizing them and by providing the special conditions they require to display their talent in fullness. Heaven has sent us super-talented children for our benefit and inspiration, and they too need nurturing. We perceive the result of extraordinary talent differently: as natural perfection, beauty, or awe-inspiring; often overwhelming and unstoppable against the odds. The examples are numerous and uniquely interesting. Let's briefly look at three examples.

Wolfgang Amadeus Mozart's father, Leopold, was a musician and quickly discovered that his son was musically gifted and concluded that he would change music history.[19] Later in life, many of Leopold's friends would comment on how brilliant and quick to learn young Wolfgang was. Mozart's prodigious abilities were always evident. We could almost say that Mozart was born knowing how to play music (nature) and grew up under Leopold's intensive instruction (nurture). When he was four years old, he began playing the piano. By the tender age of five, Mozart could read and write music —and entertain people with his skills on the keyboard. By the time he turned six, he had written his first compositions and composed a symphony by the time he was eight.[20] At age eight, while visiting London in 1764, he surprised Daines Barrington with his abilities. The Englishman wrote of the young composer: "He began to play the symphony in a most masterly manner." [21] Some very prestigious guests were amazed at how accomplished he was.

2) Helen Keller was not only affected by severe disabilities, but she also overcame them. Helen became deaf and blind at 19 months due to an attack of scarlet fever. In the fragment that follows from a biography, we can appreciate the interplay between nature and nurture:

"Keller's parents requested that a teacher from the Perkins Institution in Boston, Massachusetts, be sent to instruct the child soon thereafter. Anne M. Sullivan was sent to Helen's home in Tuscumbia, Alabama, to train her according to the methods of Dr. Samuel Gridley Howe. From 1888 onwards, at the Perkins Institution, and under Sarah Fuller at the Horace Mann School in New York, she learned to read, write, and talk, and became proficient to some degree in the ordinary education curriculum, several languages, and mathematics. In 1900, Keller entered Radcliffe College. With the aid of Anne Sullivan and other tutors, she took a full program of 17 1/2 courses including Mathematics, Latin, French, German, English, and History, and graduated cum laude in 1904. After her college education, Keller began working extensively in causes for people who are blind in the United States and internationally." [22]

Helen's autobiography, *The Story of My Life*,[23] published in 1903; and translated into 50 languages, is recognized as one of the most extraordinary autobiographies ever written.

3) José Raúl Capablanca was a Cuban regarded as one of the greatest chess players in history.[24] His talent was recognized when he was four years old (nature) by pointing out his father's illegal move during the game and then beating him at the game! The child was then regularly exposed to the game by his father (nurture). The talent shown by the child was so perplexing that his family took him to a brain surgeon. The doctor diagnosed Capablanca as having extraordinary mental power for a boy his age and advised him not to play chess. Fortunately for chess lovers, the boy was allowed to play again not long after. It is very instructive what Capablanca wrote years later about his first exposure to a chess board and the game:

"I approached closer, and obtained my first view of a chess-board. Without disturbing the silence that prevailed, I took a position at the table, where I could view the proceedings comfortably. My boyish curiosity soon grew to wonder; and very shortly, after observing how my father was moving those peculiarly shaped figures from square to square of the board, I felt a sudden fascination for the game. The impression came upon me that this curious game must have a military significance, judging from the interest the two soldiers manifested. I then began to concentrate my mind on discovering how the pieces should be moved; and at the conclusion of the first game I felt sure that I had learned the rules for the movement of chessmen. A second game was played. By this time the wonder of an "Arabian Nights" tale could not have held me more. I followed each move eagerly. Having solved the first mystery of chess – the movement of the pieces – I sought to find out the principles that underlie the game. Although I was only four years old at the time, I could soon appreciate the fact that a game of chess may be compared to a military battle – something that involves an attack on the part of one player, and a defense on the part of another. Action of this nature always made a deep impression upon me. I recall with what delight I used to listen to a soldier's story of the capture of a redoubt or the trapping of an army. I believe, therefore, that my early and very strong attraction to the game of chess was due to the peculiar set of mind that I had developed as a result of my military environment, and also to a peculiar intuition...It is not correct to assume, however, that my chess ability depends upon an overdeveloped memory. In chess, memory may be an aid, but it is not indispensable. At the present time my memory is far from what it was in my early youth, yet my play is undoubtedly much stronger than it was then. Mastery of chess and brilliance of play do not depend so much upon the memory as upon the peculiar functioning of the powers of the brain."[25]

LONG-TERM BENEFITS OF LOVE

Scientific Evidence

In the past, much research on childhood history of health has centered on identifying risk factors for illness. These included things like parental neglect and parental abuse. However, by comparison, positive aspects that may help promote health and well-being in later life were relatively understudied. In recent times such a limited approach has been changing. The examples that follow will illustrate this new perspective. "Parental warmth and flourishing in mid-life"[26,27] is a study title in recent years. The Human Flourishing Program at Harvard University conducted this study. Flourishing is a technical term used by academics and philosophers. The word meaning is similar to "happiness." Human flourishing, "well-being," or a "good life," conveys a close-enough sense for the layperson.

The study revealed that people's early relationship with their parents has a strong and positive influence on their emotional, psychological, and social well-being well into mid-life. Prior research on parental warmth has analyzed its impact on individual aspects of well-being. However, the Harvard study's new contribution to understanding this topic is its examination of parental affection concerning multiple measures of flourishing. The association between flourishing and parental warmth was strong even when considering other childhood factors; parental warmth early in life is linked to well-being in multiple areas later in mid-life. Parental warmth is also inversely related to unhealthy behavior outcomes such as drug abuse and smoking. This Harvard study suggests the value of targeting parenting to improve population health. Among those factors are socioeconomic status and familial religiousness.

Findings like this and many others are valuable for public health and families. We should not be prompt to discard time-proven traditional values in terms of policies. While the world around us changes rapidly, our biology does not. In terms of public policy, targeting parenting to improve population health has social and economic value. For instance, using resources now dedicated to treating illness could help promote social improvement in other areas. Encouraging an approach that starts at the foundation of society is essential. Cultivating a warm family environment and affectionate parenting can have dramatic outcomes on the happiness and well-being of individuals later in life.

For many parents, this finding will not come as a surprise. Traditionally, it has been common knowledge that a parent's love goes a long way. How much will it affect a child's future well-being and health? The answer is more than previously thought by researchers. The revalue of love should be good news; our culture needs to refocus on this traditional persuasion of perennial value. As parents, we desire to bring up children who grow up to live in a good World. We hope that they grow and learn and contribute to society. We wish them to have a sense of purpose in their life. We want them to navigate the experiences and challenges of the World with positive attitudes and emotions. In a word, we want them to live fulfilling and satisfying lives.

In another long-term study, Duke University Medical School followed five hundred people from early childhood until their early 30s.[28] Researchers found that babies with affectionate and attentive mothers grow up to be happier, more resilient, and less anxious adults. Psychologists tested the babies when they were eight months old and registered the mothers' interactions with them. Researchers interviewed the same individuals 30 years later and asked about their emotional health. The adults whose mothers did not hold back affection were much less likely than the others to feel anxious or stressed, hostile or psychosomatic symptoms—other results of investigations point in the same direction.[29,30] A new study from New Zealand [31,32] is causing a stir in the field of education science. The study, which followed almost 3,000 children for more than 30 years, found that self-controlled children tended to be healthier middle-aged adults, and benefits include younger brains and bodies and a better outlook on the years ahead.

A Remarkable Hormone

In the study from Duke University researchers hypothesized that one biological factor played a role.[28] The hormone oxytocin may be biologically critical for this effect, as it is released when a person feels affections related to love and connection. Oxytocin[33,34] is a substance produced in the hypothalamus—a small but vital part of the brain—and released into the bloodstream by the pituitary gland. Its primary function is to facilitate childbirth. Oxytocin directly stimulates the uterus muscles to contract and boosts the production of prostaglandins, increasing uterine contractions. Once the baby is born, oxytocin helps move milk from the ducts in the breast to the nipple. It assists in creating a bond between mother and baby.

Our bodies also produce this "magical" compound when we fall in love and are sexually excited. Hence the nickname "love hormone." Moreover, low oxytocin levels may play a role in depression, including postpartum depression.[35] Oxytocin plays a role in reward, stress, social affiliation, learning and memory processes, and behaviors related to drugs of abuse and alcohol.[36,37] Drug abuse is a significant cause of distress and dysfunction throughout the World. Acute and chronic exposure to such substances alters the oxytocin system in the brain. Studies of oxytocin continue in the context of other drugs of abuse, including cocaine, cannabis, alcohol, and methamphetamine type.[38,39,40] Its administration may reverse changes in the brain caused by drugs and alcohol use. [41,42,43]

A way to boost oxytocin naturally is with exercise.[44] One study noted a jump in oxytocin levels measured in saliva after high-intensity training.[45] Playing with children, and getting involved with them in physical activity, maybe a way of bonding and sharing our love with them with the help of oxytocin. Music also seems to have the ability to increase oxytocin levels, especially when people sing in a group.[46] Little by little, with every shared activity, we can help create boding at different levels. For instance, imagine you go to church as a family and sing together; that activity combines biological, social, and spiritual aspects of bonding that reinforce themselves to create healthier, stronger relationships. Especially if you are parents, keep in mind that the simple act of touch boosts oxytocin release; hugging your child leads to higher levels of this hormone and a greater sense of well-being and security.

Love And Stress

When a mother touches her child, she can help lower stress levels.[47,48] Researchers have found that physical contact activates certain parts of your brain that lead directly to lower levels of the stress hormone cortisol. Cortisol is a crucial hormone for a response pattern known as "fear, fight, or flight." It activates the body's resources to cope with situations of danger or extreme demands. Cortisol bears the nickname of "stress hormone." Thus, it is vital for survival, but it can cause damage to your body when persistently at high levels. For instance, chronic stress can reduce the size of the hippocampus,[49] a seahorse-shaped structure, one on each temporal lobe, under the cerebral cortex with a crucial role in memory formation and storage, emotional responses, and learning.

The brain orchestrates emotional responses in a multifaceted manner. Touch can have a calming effect as it increases endorphin levels that lower heart rate and blood pressure, and it also releases both serotonin and dopamine in the brain.[50] These neurotransmitters produce a more relaxed, calming state within our nervous system. Studies about the unique interaction between mother and baby have shed light on this. The mother's loving touch helps calm babies, so they stop crying or sleep more. Conversely, it is well-documented that children who lived in a deprived environment such as an orphanage had higher cortisol levels than those with their parents. On the other hand, nurturing children with skin-to-skin contact boosts brain development. Physical contact is a significant factor in conveying warmth and affection to a baby.

Love And Growth

As early as the fourth month in the womb, babies develop a sense of touch. A baby's first experiences of the World occur through this sense. Stimulation is essential to a child's development, and children need to be loved and touched. Touch as a way of expressing love has many positive effects on human beings. From early childhood into adulthood, touching makes us feel loved and secure and creates an attachment between parent and child. It also fosters physical, emotional, cognitive, and language development.

Physical touch is one crucial form of sharing warmth and affection with a child.[51] If you deprive a child of touch, physical and emotional growth stops even with appropriate nutrition.[52,53] Nurturing touch can improve this condition. Both releases of oxytocin and growth hormones play a role, plus other chemicals produced by the body. Growth hormones are essential for growth. Hugging and positive touch also increase other vital substances in the brain. Dopamine and serotonin are neurotransmitters that can boost your mood and relieve symptoms of depression. A study by the University of Notre Dame showed that children who received affection from their parents were happier later in life.[53]

Love And Brain Development

Touch also helps shape a child's brain development, and it can make your child smarter. Researchers from Washington University found that children lavished with affection by their mothers during the first years have a larger hippocampus.[54] This part of the brain has a vital role in learning, memory, and response to stress. The study confirms that providing children with physical care and affection can improve physical and mental development, including education.

Another study out of the University of Notre Dame confirmed previous findings.[55] Again, it showed that children who receive affection from their parents were happier as adults. A survey of hundreds of adults asked about how they were raised and, in particular, how much physical affection they received. Researchers found that those who reported receiving more love in childhood suffered less depression and anxiety and were more capable of expressing love and compassion. Conversely, those who said they received less affection battled with mental health and were less able to empathize with others.

On the other hand, childhood abuse and lack of affection negatively impact children mentally and physically. Abuse can lead to health and emotional problems throughout children's lives.[56,57] Other studies confirm that unconditional love and affection from a parent can make children emotionally happier and less anxious, and the child's brain responds positively as a result of receiving affection. Parental love could protect people against the harmful effects of childhood stress.[58]

Love And Emotional Intelligence

As we have seen, love creates a stronger parent-child bond, can make your child physically healthier, and provides your child with a sense of security and mental well-being. We also need to include the impact on your child's brain development and memory in this list of benefits. And in the areas of the brain and social development, an additional benefit: love plays a big part in developing emotional intelligence. Parental warmth and affection make your child less fearful and more adapted to the World. Researchers at Carnegie Mellon University found that physical touch plays a big part in the development of emotional intelligence.[59] It is foundational for emotional bonding and empathy. Touch is also known as a means of communicating empathy in adults. For instance, touch can help relieve pain in medical care settings. We tend to touch a part of our body that is in pain. We all have experienced this instinctive behavior. We exchange hugs for sharing comfort and strength when we lose a family member or a friend.

LOVE IN ACTION

Touch

Showing affection for your child through physical contact and hugging is essential. For babies, it is as vital as milk. Skin-to-skin contact is like nutrition for your baby. When parents are home with the newborn child, they should hold, touch, rock, talk, and sing to the baby. At this early stage, communication is essential to provide affection to your child. Hugging has a place throughout childhood and beyond. The younger the child, the more parents will hug them. A big hug can do wonders for a child accustomed to receiving affection; it will become something natural. Hugs can be very comforting during times of high emotion. They bring reassurance and security. Find what duration and strength are best according to the child's desire and response.

Laughter

Humor can be beneficial to children. It not only stimulates different body systems, but also decreases levels of stress hormones like cortisol and epinephrine and increases the activation of the dopamine reward system in the brain.[60,61] The happiest, most integrated families laugh together. Cuddling is another way to show affection. Just wrap your arms around your child and relax together. Then, tickling can be a fun way to be silly and laugh together. Creating opportunities for laughter is a natural and effective way to share warmth and affection. As a touch, laughter helps you bind with your child through biological responses like those previously mentioned. Affirm laughter in your children; you may say things like, "your laughter is one of the great things about you." Laughter stimulates endorphins and oxytocin in both you and your child. Laughter creates a virtuous cycle. First, our brains build memory pathways based on happy emotional experiences. As a result, the more happy memories you share with your child, the more they will tend to see you in a positive light. This good image of you will contribute to a healthy self-image of themselves. And keep in mind, there is more to those experiences than biology. We will touch on this in chapter 5.

Opportunities to act silly are endless. Acting silly can make your child giggle with the same effect as laughter. Making funny faces, imitating the sound of animals, dancing humorously, or walking comically, you will make your child giggle or laugh. You can also add "silly actions" to your repertoire for dealing with situations that may require some discipline or correction. At first, the child may laugh but then understand that something isn't right. There are many other ways to show love through touch, such as hand holding, a high five, handshakes, running together, etc. Eventually, you will find what your child likes best. One more thing, kids love using made-up words. Use nonsense words and see how your child responds.

Playful Parenting

As the child grows, the range of activities will expand; parents can be playful in many ways, from creating silly games to doing fun activities like dancing together. Playing with your child is an excellent way to share time. It is also an opportunity to teach your child new skills, share laughter, and relax. But there is more to play. Playing is a way for children to keep active and be happy. Freely chosen play helps children develop healthily. To have physical and mental health while learning life skills, they need various unstructured play opportunities throughout their childhood.

Playing is a way for children to explore the World and naturally learn about themselves, and they also learn and develop skills they need for study, work, and relationships. Experts in this field recognize the importance of play for such aspects as confidence, self-esteem, resilience, personal interaction, social skills, independence, and coping with challenging situations. Play is an excellent way to help the child explore the World, imagine scenarios, assume roles, and express their natural curiosity.

Playful parenting [62,63] helps parents fully bond with their children while having fun. Adults can support and participate in their child's play activities during early childhood games. However, they should not always direct what happens. You must give your children time, freedom, and choice to play. If an adult makes all the decisions—how, what, and when their child plays—children will not enjoy their play experiences.

Service And Gratefulness

Service and gratefulness should go together. We cannot live happy, fulfilled lives without gratitude. Love requires training your child on these two aspects. Doing so is a productive way to show a child love and affection. Service is love in action. There can be endless opportunities to show love through small acts of service. Find out your child's favorite foods and surprise them from time to time with a special treat. At the same time, teach them how to make it themselves. You want them to be self-reliant in the future. Point out the acts of service you do and give opportunity for your child's participation. For example, you could point out that you cook a meal for their nourishment and enjoyment and have the child put the dishes away. If the child has a particular chore, you could have them give you a hand to finish it and show gratitude. If your child has completed a project, you may appreciate a job well done. Create every opportunity to emphasize the importance of service and appreciation. Make your child understand that a more significant purpose exists in life beyond themselves. A word of caution, discipline, and love go together. Parents should not be permissive and give in to every request. The child needs to understand that parents are not the child's servants. Use your service to the child as an example and teach them to show their gratitude.

Affirmation Through Words

Recognizing a child's efforts can help instill confidence and encourage them to apply themselves to learn and achieve. Instead of making general statements, be specific. Rather than just saying, "you are so intelligent," you may also say, "I liked the effort you made to finish your project even when it was hard." Never diminish your child in conversation with other people, especially when they can overhear. Instead, let your child overhear you telling someone about some good quality you see in them or something great they did. Like, "David was very kind at school today, and he lifted his friend when she fell. I am impressed with him!" Affirmations like this can have a lasting positive effect on your child, and it will help him internalize that good quality as his.

Your child should not perceive your love as being conditional. For example, do not use phrases like "I love you when you behave well." Saying "I love what you did…" is different. "I love you no matter what" is a phrase they need to hear. Above all, they need to perceive it and feel it, even when it is not said. "My son, I believe in you" is a powerful phrase that will plant a seed of necessary confidence in themselves. If you are a believer, you let your child know that she is precious, created after God's image. It is also important to tell them: "My daughter, you are unique!". Their uniqueness and value as a person, different from any other person who has ever lived, is something they should hear—their uniqueness and their understanding that there is more to life than themselves should go together. Infuse them with a sense of a larger purpose. Life is not all about themselves. Life is larger and more exciting than that! There are things to be discovered, missions to be accomplished, people that will need our help, and a larger purpose for living.

Instilling trust in your child is nothing but an expression of love. Let your child know that they can tell you anything. Reiterate phrases like "I will love you no matter what." Ask questions such as "Tell me about what you are doing" and say, "I love spending time with you." Cultivate a bonding of trust and confidentiality. This way, you also help your child develop decision-making capacity. Let them know that their choices are important, and they matter. When you say, "I am proud of the person you are becoming," you encapsulate in one phrase all their good qualities and achievements until that point in time. "You are a great daughter" and "You are a great son" have a similar effect. Trust also can be projected into the future. "You will be a great mother," "Your will be a great father," "You will be good as a leader," and other similar phrases. Allow me to share an anecdote in memory of my parents. My mother said to me more than once, in my father's presence, when you were a baby, green grasshoppers (popularly called Esperanzas, the word for hope in Spanish) came to your mosquito net and covered your cradle. When you become a man, you will be a messenger of hope. Those affirming words were telling the child: you will grow up to be a man of goodwill. Never underestimate the power of seeds planted with love in a child's soul.

Love Through Language

Just as young children need nourishing food for physical growth, they also need linguistic nutrition. Talking to them is extremely important for developing language and cognitive abilities. Talking to toddlers boosts their language skills while conveying affection.[64] New research from Stanford psychologists shows that by talking more to their toddler, parents help the child learn to process language more quickly, which accelerates vocabulary growth. Introduce new words from daily life regularly according to age. For example, when you look at a color or an object, repeat the word to the child. You may present the child with different things of the same color. As the child develops and you introduce new words, you may try to explain this word with the help of practical examples. Concrete examples will help them generalize the meaning of words. If you visit the doctor, you may talk to the child about what a physician does, how they are helpful, etc. This way, you will help your child understand the correct usage and interpret the word's right meaning. Words, images, actions, and context will enhance learning and feed a child's natural curiosity. Do not forget to use funny words, which will add enjoyment and laughter and facilitate learning new words.

Reading

Tell your child stories and read to them daily. Use language and books according to their age. Did you know that reading to your children can help them learn to read? A study in the Journal of Developmental and Behavioral Pediatrics [65] found that young children whose parents read them one picture book a day provide their children with exposure to an estimated 78,000 words each year during story time. They enter kindergarten having heard many more words than kids who did not have the same opportunity.

According to Jessica Logan, lead author of the study and assistant professor of educational studies at The Ohio State University, this gap in exposure to spoken words could be one key in explaining differences in vocabulary and reading development. According to her, children who are read one book a day, by age 5, will hear many more words than those who don't regularly read books with a parent or caregiver. "Kids who hear more vocabulary words will be better prepared to see those words in print when they enter school," said Logan. Researchers have concluded that children are likely to pick up reading skills more quickly and efficiently when they start school. As we move on to other chapters, we will see how discipline, freedom, and instruction work better on the solid foundation of love. First, let's look at the importance of the family as a functional unit.

The Family Together

We now live in an era of pervasive self-absorbing distractions, screen time, and social media. It is a paradox that many of us have become less social. We now have access to many beneficial opportunities for learning and growth.[66] Social connections are essential for your well-being, but you need solid, healthy relationships to reap their full benefits. However, we should guard against relationships that are not healthy for our children's mental and physical well-being. Some types of social connections appear to be more beneficial than others, and we need in-person interactions to reap the full benefits from our social network of relationships. For instance, according to a study from the American "Journal of Health Promotion," excessive social media usage is one of the most significant risk factors for loneliness.[67]

Humans are social beings, and connections with other people are essential. Before we move on, consider the numerous benefits of healthy social relationships.[68-70] Social links can help you live longer and build a more fulfilling life. Having strong social connections increases your longevity, improves your life satisfaction, and helps protect you from mental and physical illness. Connection to others also enables you to cope with trauma, recover from illness, and bounce back from stress-related setbacks. Cultivate relationships that would support you in growing your spiritual life. Social connection can reduce loneliness, stress, and anxiety and motivate you to take care of yourself. Conversely, it's easy to lose motivation when you feel isolated, become more depressed or anxious, or sick. More friendly people tend to live longer than those who prefer to be alone.[71]

Social connections don't just keep us happier and reduce stress but also significantly impact our longevity.[72] A meta-analysis of 148 studies analyzing data from more than 300,000 participants found that more socially connected people have a 50% lower mortality risk.[73] In other words, being more sociable can increase your life expectancy by seven to nine years! The benefits of social connection include building a solid foundation for our children to have enough quality social interaction. But why is social relationship so effective in keeping us healthier? Why do we live longer when we spend time with others? Several theories attempt to explain this phenomenon:

- Social connections offer support against stressors. Stress is a significant contributor to disease and having a solid network of friends or family helps you manage stressful situations better. This improved ability to handle stress can significantly improve outcomes for chronic diseases such as heart disease and diabetes—and may even help you avoid them in the first place!

- Social connections make us feel secure and safe. Feeling safe allows our bodies to relax, which reduces wear and tear on our tissues and inflammation levels—both factors contribute to aging faster and developing diseases such as cancer or heart disease earlier in life.

- Social connections make us feel valued by others, strengthening a sense of self-worth and contributing to overall feelings of happiness and satisfaction with life—all things that boost your immune system function!

The same is true for children: kids who have strong social bonds with their parents are less prompt to get involved in drugs or crime and do better in school. Children's emotional development depends on having a solid bond with their parents. When children are loved by their parents, they can better explore the world around them without fear of being vulnerable or mistreated by others.

When it comes to relationships quality is paramount, more than the number of family members or friends you have. For a child, being able to confide in at least one family member or a close friend is essential. A bad close relationship can be worse than no close relationship at all. For example, a bad relationship can cause stress and anxiety, leading to depression and other mental illnesses.

On the other hand, a healthy family environment can be the best place to foster social connections in your child's life. They will incorporate patterns that will guide them throughout their lives. Thus, while a social link is essential for your well-being, you need solid and healthy relationships to reap their full benefits. A similar principle applies to your child's education in this area. Some types of social connections appear to be more beneficial than others. Family relationships should have a preeminent place of importance; friends are also important as other types of positive relationships. The influence of friends and peers becomes very significant during the teenage years, hence the importance of establishing a solid foundation in the early years of a child's life.

Being around supportive people can help you manage stress better.[74] A supportive family will have a similar effect on the child.

Small acts of kindness can increase your happiness. Having children participate in such an act will positively impact both parents and children.[75] Think in ways you can have your child involved in helping others. Doing something every day makes it easier to do. Make a habit of participating in small acts of kindness with your child. There is something psychologically and spiritually special behind the saying that "there is more happiness in giving than receiving." These and other principles will direct your child to the quality of being magnanimous. Magnanimous is an English word that comes from Latin. It means having a large soul. According to The American Heritage® Dictionary of the English Language,[76] the term has meanings such as "Highly moral, especially in showing kindness or forgiveness, as in overlooking insults or not seeking revenge"; "Great of mind; elevated in soul or in sentiment; raised above what is low, mean, or ungenerous; of lofty and courageous spirit" and "Dictated by or exhibiting nobleness of soul; honorable; noble; not selfish." Little by little, as a family, you can lead the child to live according to high standards and ideals.

Teach the child the importance of being able to spend time alone. At the same time, help them find the balance of being able to spend time with other people without feeling like they need to be alone or using screen time or social media. Having healthy relationships means feeling comfortable spending time alone and with others. Teach them about the advantages of having a family. Children who have a family tend to be happier and more satisfied.[77] Studies have shown that families that spend time together experience less stress and anxiety and live a healthier lifestyle. The family can give children motivation to be the best version of themselves. Why is doing things together as a family so important? Family activities together create lasting patterns of pathways in the brain, memories, and positive experiences cemented by love and support. Being with family helps construct life principles and improves overall mental health, adaptability, and resilience. Family members can coach each other to help navigate life's ups and downs. Family is what makes us who we are.

Family Meals

Did you know that family meals are more than good food and conversation? Studies show that children who eat with their families at least three times a week are better adjusted, do better in school, and are less likely to smoke, drink, or use drugs.[78,79] That's the actual value. The time you spend together at the dining table may be one of the essential times spent in your day. In a world where life is busy, enjoying family meals together means sharing special moments and creating memories that will last a lifetime. Studies [80] have also shown that sharing nutritious meals prepares children for success in school, healthy eating, and forming good habits as they grow.

Family meals positively contribute to children's physical and mental development, nutritional status, and health-related behaviors. Children who sat down at regular family meals are less likely to exhibit negative behaviors, including substance abuse and violence. Many studies show that when children share family meals, they tend to be healthier, happier, and better in school. Family meals are a chance to catch up and find out what's going on while ensuring everyone gets the nutrients they need. There's nothing like family mealtime to bring family and friends closer together, from toddlers to teens. Benefits are real, as shown in a new study from Harvard University, eating together as a family has multiple benefits for children of all ages.[81,82]

Family meals create a foundation for many other activities as a family. The list is endless, from going for regular walks, going for a long walk or a hike, playing hide and seek, watching a movie, playing a board game, and attending a sports event. You may also do other simple things that will be a novelty for your child. For instance, start a lemonade stand, write a thank you letter to a friend or family member, read a new book together, drive to some unknown place, start a hobby, and exercise together. Whatever you do, enjoy the simple pleasures in life with your children. The family will enjoy it, and it will be well worthy!

DISCIPLINE

"Do not train a child to learn by force or harshness; but direct them to it by what amuses their minds, so that you may be better able to discover with accuracy the peculiar bent of the genius of each."
—*Plato, The Republic* [15]

Children need boundaries. They want a world where they know what is right and wrong, safe and unsafe. They need consistency so that they can feel in control. Boundaries help ensure safety for children and guide them towards becoming sensible adults. Children need to know what's acceptable behavior and what's not. They may feel confused about the right actions if you let them get away with everything. The media will happily encourage your children to do things you don't want them to do, like swearing and drinking alcohol. Parents can provide training for their children by teaching them how to behave by setting boundaries and behavioral expectations. Limits give children control over their little world, making them feel safer. Discipline is an essential part of education. Like all iconic poets, José Martí—the Cuban luminary, writer, and patriot—said it best: "There is happiness in duty, although it may not seem so. To fulfill one's duty elevates the soul to a state of constant sweetness. Love is the bond between men, the way to teach, and the center of the World."[83]

It's not about neglecting freedom – it's about making sure that

· DISCIPLINE ·

your child is in a position to learn and grow. When children are disciplined, they tend to become more self-disciplined by nature. Discipline is often mistakenly understood as punishment and, in the case of the home, often abandoned. Changes in culture have contributed to this decline in discipline, including the idea that discipline equals punishment, abuse, permissiveness, and bad temper. Discipline should be positive and based on respect, encouragement, and nurturing. There is little evidence to support the use of punitive or regret-focused discipline. Research provides clear evidence that punitive parents are not as effective at promoting and maintaining self-discipline in their children.[84-86]

Discipline may be tried and tested, but that doesn't mean it's old school. Discipline is a pillar of parenting; it can be fun with love and the right mindset. Give your children room to learn from their mistakes, but always be there to guide them through them. Do not shelter them from failure, but instead help them when they need it most. Our responsibility is to follow their growth and become better parents and role models for our children. It is easy to think that discipline is something you may do when children are wayward or are not listening and following the guidelines of your home. The truth is the opposite. Discipline comes from the Latin word 'discipulus,' meaning pupil. That implies that it is something you must learn, yet the reality is that most of us did not train on how to control our actions or behaviors. Discipline is simply training your mind, body, and spirit to behave appropriately in different situations. Discipline is about educating your child to learn and be prepared for life. Discipline can start with waking up, going to bed, and eating at certain times of the day.

According to The American Heritage® Dictionary of the English Language,[76] the word discipline has several meanings; for this book, the following will suffice:

"n. 1. Training expected to produce a specific character or pattern of behavior, especially training that produces moral or mental improvement

(...)

tr.v. dis·ci·plined, dis·ci·plin·ing, dis·ci·plines

1. To train by instruction and practice, as in following rules or developing self-control: The sergeant disciplined the recruits to become soldiers. See Synonyms at teach.

2. To punish in order to gain control or enforce obedience. See Synonyms at punish.

3. To impose order on: needed to discipline their study habits.

[Middle English, from Old French descepline, from Latin disciplīna, from discipulus, pupil; see DISCIPLE.]"

Each aspect applies to the role of discipline in a child's education. Research shows that discipline is crucial in helping children control their behavior. The challenge for parents, and educators in general, is to find the right balance between structure and flexibility, freedom and responsibility so that children can become productive citizens who make a positive contribution to society. Well-disciplined children rely more on developing self-discipline in their teenage years and are better at independent thinking and decision-making. They are more likely to complete school, succeed at university and develop reliable social networks.[87-89]

Discipline is a way for parents to teach their children about the world and develop their characters. When applied effectively, it offers parents many benefits, such as modifying children's behavior, developing mental health, and building a strong relationship with their child. As we will see throughout the chapters of this book, love, discipline, freedom, and instruction can and need to work together so the seeds we plant in our children's life can grow on fertile ground and produce abundant fruits. This chapter outlines some tips and ideas on using discipline to educate better and nurture your child. We can't give our children wings, but we ought to teach them how to use them. Children need structure and sturdiness around them, a sense of discipline and stability, to propel them into the World. Without these things, they cannot learn to thrive. Raising a child becomes a school of discipline for parents too. Discipline should support all other areas to build an intellectual, physical, and moral personality and develop their eventual talents.

Discipline, love, and freedom provide room for trial and error, allowing children to learn from their mistakes, but always be there to guide them through. Do not overly shelter them from failure, but instead help them through it. Disciplining a child is complicated and as much as we would like to think that it's one-size-fits-all, it's not. There are many variables: Is the child a firstborn or later born? What is the child's temperament? What works for one child will probably not work for another. I know that discipline is much more than controlling your child's behavior. Staying in control is just as crucial for the adult as for the child. You want to say yes a lot and no when you need to. A little discipline will go a long way, instead of yelling, try de-escalating the situation with a sense of humor. More than a super-nanny advocate, this is a guide to help parents with the basics and more specific problems. It aspires to give them a new way of seeing things by focusing on fundamental principles.

No matter what your age is, parenting is a stressful time in your life. You've got a lot of advice, but you'd like to know if there is any scientific evidence supporting what you do or will do to educate your child. It is helpful to understand how you can benefit from managing your child's behavior, learning, and development. It is also very gratifying for parents. Since the beginning of time, parents have been disciplining their children to ensure they would grow to be adults. Now more than ever, with the new dangers that children face in modern times, discipline plays an integral role in keeping them safe. A balanced approach will help you learn how to discipline your child effectively. Disciplining a child is an opportunity to mold them into better people and a foundation for their future lives as grown-ups. With these helpful discipline ideas, you'll be able to improve your children's behavior while making sure they grow up with proper communication skills and interact nicely with others.

Everyone from your great aunt to strangers you meet in line at the grocery store has an opinion on discipline and raising kids. Today, things are different from when dad's word was law and "children should be seen, not heard." But that doesn't mean we have to throw the baby out with the bathwater. The truth is discipline does make a difference in how children grow up—and it's not so that they can behave better in public or get good grades (although those are important too). Now, let us consider the keys to effective discipline and illustrate how to use them appropriately. A scientifically backed overview exists for the methods of discipline that we will now discuss. These approaches highlight the benefits of discipline as a pillar of education regarding your child's present and future life achievements.

Effective Discipline

The role of discipline includes using strategies such as positive reinforcement to encourage good behavior, gentle encouragement that is not condescending and teaching coping strategies and problem-solving skills. Principles of self-determination theory[90] and explaining to children why particular behaviors are inappropriate can support those strategies. These strategies may also encourage the child to take control of their behavior or actions. Before we investigate those strategies, let us first consider what makes discipline effective. An article published in the "Journal of Pediatrics and Child Health,"[91] reveals essential clues to effective discipline, it needs to be:

1. Given by an adult with an emotional bond to the child
2. Consistent, close to the behavior needing change
3. Perceived as 'fair' by the child
4. Developmentally and temperamentally appropriate
5. Self-enhancing and leading to self-discipline

An Adult with A Love Bond to The Child

The role of discipline has been well-researched, and the results are indisputable. For example, K. Maccoby & J. Martin[92] write, "Effective Discipline is a function of an affective bond with the adult. If a child has a positive emotional tie to an adult, he will be responsive to that person's control." Discipline is a method of teaching a child self-control. We need to administer discipline in the context of an affective bond with either parent or teacher to be effective. Any well-researched review of the scientific literature would show the importance of discipline in supporting child development. Disciplining should be used assertively, with a calm and firm tone, and in a way that conveys respect for the child. An adult should only give discipline that the child trusts to be fair, consistent, and reasonable.

If your child is acting like he just crawled out from under a rock, it sounds like you need to lay down some discipline. We're all for consequences in the form of time-outs and taking away privileges. But it would help if you were the disciplinarian—not a sibling or a nanny. And if your discipline is going to have an effect, you've got to be emotionally connected to your child. If you're nasty regularly, or your children don't know where they stand with you, they won't take your corrections seriously—or they'll learn the wrong lessons from them.

Conscientious parents know they'll be more successful if they run their households like a well-oiled machine. And that's not just good advice—it's science: children do best when adults love and care for them and when rules and routines surround them. For example, as a toddler parent, you are probably well-versed in discipline, as we all need to be. Discipline may include various practices such as time-outs, reward systems, and chore charts.

Consistency

Did you know that discipline is more about consistency than anything else? Discipline requires consistency, and at the same time, it creates it. Not surprisingly, one of the precious fruits of discipline is, you guessed, consistency! In this age of permissive society where children are allowed to run wild, it is good to know how to be consistent in our discipline if we have children. This book will help you with that!

Both consistency and proximity are key to training children effectively. Discipline is about teaching self-control, not punishment. It shouldn't be doled out as an afterthought when a child does something wrong. Think of it as training rather than punishment—it's what you do before the problem happens. Good discipline is more about consistency than quantity. Crucial to effective discipline is not only "when" you give it, but "how" and "why." Most importantly, look at the types of consequences you provide when constructing your approach to discipline while deciding on your rules, and sticking to them.

Being consistent means, you follow through on your rules and consequences every time your child breaks a rule. Discipline needs to be compatible with all children. Of course, children will behave differently at different ages and stages of development, and your disciplinary measures should fit with what your child can understand. Being consistently fair to your kids — day after day, week after week, month after month — lets them know that you love them and will do whatever it takes to help them keep on track. If you let rules slide when convenient for you, your children will learn that there will be no consequence if they can wait it out. Consistency can bring security to a child. If Mom says it, it must be true, right? Try to stay on the same page as your child's other caregiver so that his discipline is uniform and predictable.

Parents who are inconsistent in enforcing rules for their children will likely have difficulty controlling their behavior. But parents who are too harsh—or strict without explaining reasons—may be able to influence behavior for a time. But the child's feelings of anger and resentment may only simmer below the surface and cause problems later. Keep punishments and rewards consistent. If discipline is harsh and inconsistent, your children may develop feelings of guilt, become distrustful and defiant, or depend too much on others for direction. If you see your child is not following the rule, remind him or her again. When they follow the rules, praise them for following them. That you are serious about your rules needs to be clear to your children.

You may set up a "reward system." It works like this:

1. Tell your children that every time they do what you say or follow a rule, they get a reward (whatever small reward you decide).

2. Note that discipline will be more effective if your children get involved in establishing the rules. If there is a need to change them, talk about it to your child before breaking the rule.

3. Experiment with different strategies to find the ones that work for you and your family.

4. Remember that as your children grow, they become ready for changes in rules and limits, be flexible.

Close to the Behavior Needing Change

If you want to use discipline as a means of encouraging your children to become more responsible and mature, then you must make sure that the discipline is applied quickly and with a direct connection to the behavior. Simply put, the longer you wait, the less likely it is that you will be able to discipline with any strength of the effect. Letting your child get away with bad behavior just once can become ingrained into his or her habitual responses and make life harder for everyone.

Use ways of acting and disciplinary measures proportional to the behavior and attitude problems that need to be corrected. Granted, discipline in a family can be tricky. However, disproportionate reactions will help neither you nor your child. A child needs teaching and training that is fair and proportionate to the situation. Time outs and detentions should not be severe or long-lasting just because something may be hard for you to handle. Your children will learn as they see you apply self-control. A child needs to understand the values you want to teach. These values include learning respect for authority and others, self-discipline, and honesty. It should be abundantly clear that love does not have to equal spoiling or allowing children to avoid discipline. They are still developing the ability for self-discipline. Remember that you need to be flexible in disciplining for the best results. The perfect mother or father is an ideal, but the pursuit of perfection can at least provide direction and guiding principles.

What does it mean to discipline your child proportionately? Simply put, the reaction must be equal to the action. If you scream and yell at a kid for leaving his shoes in the middle of the hallway, he will figure out that it is difficult to gain approval when it comes to sitting still during dinner or picking up his room, so he might choose to disobey those rules too. Remember that every child is different. The same disciplinary approach does not work for every child. But these are two things that apply to every child. First, the reaction should fit the offense. Second, don't overreact! Never punish your child without thinking ahead of time about how you will respond and why. If you decide what consequences are appropriate, accomplishing your goals will be easier. Keep calm when implementing rules, take time to see the effectiveness of each result, and adjust accordingly.

Perceived As 'Fair' By the Child

Parenting requires courage, fairness, and a sense of justice. You must be in control of yourself when reacting to an undisciplined child. Do not yell at the child like a drill sergeant barking orders to a squad of raw recruits. When disciplining your child, bear in mind that parents must also be fair in applying rules and teaching discipline. First and foremost, it is worth repeating, be fair with your child. Children don't like being disciplined by their parents. If you feel that your discipline was incorrect while growing up, why repeat the same mistakes with your child?

These are some points to always keep in mind:

(1) Do not shout and yell at the child when he does something wrong (this will undermine his perception of fair treatment).

(2) Do not be afraid of disciplining your child, i.e., treat them with equal respect to establish authority in a kindhearted manner.

(3) Start early in your child's life and be consistent to avoid creating negative habits.

(4) Do not mistreat your children.

(5) Do not spank your child. It will not teach them what you want them to learn, but it will lead them to be angry. Spanking communicates anger rather than love.

Developmentally and Temperamentally Appropriate

Discipline should be developmentally and temperamentally appropriate. Appropriate means that instead of the same rules applied to everyone, you customize it to fit the child's unique needs. It goes a lot further than just age, so let us keep that in mind! Children develop differently; some are shy and quiet, while others are bolder and more aggressive. It wouldn't be fair nor effective to use the same strategies for all children as it wouldn't address their individual needs. Watch how your child reacts to particular methods and change them accordingly. Be Flexible!

You've probably heard that there is no one-size-fits-all approach to discipline. The reason is simple: what works for a four-year-old won't work for a 10-year-old. So how do we know the best way to discipline our child? Here's where understanding "temperament" comes in. Let's face it, parenting is tough, and being disciplined is probably one of the hardest things about it, especially if your child's personality type and temperament are different than yours.

Self-Enhancing Quality

We all desire our children to become respected people, successful in life. We want them to have a strong sense of right and wrong, to be helpful and unselfish. We want them to know how to work hard, persevere, achieve goals and make wise choices. These accomplishments don't just happen; they will learn these life skills as part of a process. That's where self-enhancing discipline comes in. Discipline should be self-enhancing means that be ultimately leading to self-discipline. When we decide to live a life of self-discipline and follow it, we begin to build our character. We begin to gain valuable qualities that help us resist temptations and live the good life that we have envisioned. Self-discipline is a form of freedom. It develops your inner freedom from weakness and dependence on emotions. If we were to give a definition of self-discipline, it would go something like this: A commitment to a personal decision you make that shapes and defines your character and creates patterns of behavior that will help you achieve your goals.

We tend to spend all our energy and time by overloading ourselves with useless information in the information age. One of the goals of self-enhancing discipline is to protect our children against a waste of energy and talent by wasting their potential in an undisciplined manner. Remember that self-discipline, the ability to cultivate self-control, is the most important factor affecting success in any field. Discipline is a critical life skill, and without it, we cannot get any work done.

But let's be serious: do we want to force our children to work hard and become smart? Of course not! We want them to have fun, enjoy themselves, make mistakes while learning, and achieve great things, as in stories where magic wands turn kids into geniuses who save the World! One needs the discipline, of course, but we are not talking about that kind of discipline here—the kind that makes perfect people—no, we are talking about self-enhancing discipline! It's the kind that makes people more disciplined by itself—like the notable self-cleaning ovens or dishwashers, which clean themselves automatically after every use.

Put yourself on your child's foot as he develops. We can think of this kind of discipline as having three levels. They are not strictly sequential, as different brain parts develop in parallel and interact with each other. The first level is understanding what you will do, such capacity is enhanced by the time a child is learning how to read and not just how to speak. This ability will help the child use other skills more efficiently, such as listening or writing. The second level is being able to organize yourself with these skills and make plans based on them. In this case, discipline would include being able to use language as a tool to guide your behavior effectively. Finally, discipline means being able to master your own body. Self-control is a vital part of this process, allowing you to control your emotions and desires so that they do not control you at inappropriate times.

Types of Discipline

Before mentioning types of discipline, a word about parenting styles, psychologists and educators have classified them with terms like uninvolved, permissive, strict, overbearing, authoritative, neglectful, and authoritarian. Our purpose is to emphasize a balanced parenting style that does not fit in those categories. This balanced approach will allow you to flow with versatility and flexibility to apply different styles according to the child's personality, age, situation, etc. Let's talk now about types of disciplines based on different philosophies of education.

Positive Discipline

Positive discipline's foundation lies in respect, an essential element of any healthy relationship.[93-95] When parents and educators treat children with dignity and respect, it goes a long way in teaching them. The positive discipline focuses on the positive rather than the negative. It might seem more straightforward to tell your child what they are doing wrong; however, you can help your child develop self-control and make good choices by praising them when they're doing something right. Positive discipline teaches your child valuable life skills such as problem-solving and conflict resolution skills. When you support your child, you're helping them become a mature, responsible adult who has healthy self-esteem and can control their behavior.

This type of discipline praises and encourages. In positive discipline, parents often help the child find a sense of belonging in the world around them and teach them problem-solving skills to help them tackle the situation when they do not behave properly. Positive discipline relies on mutual respect where parents sit and talk to their little ones whenever they make mistakes. The primary key to positive discipline is to teach children effectively without making them feel bad. The objective is to teach the child to learn from his mistakes, so he does not repeat them. Positive discipline is firm and assertive but not punishing, and it relies more on honesty and fairness than on natural authority.

Discipline is more than simply teaching your child to behave; it teaches social and life skills. Discipline is often confused with punishment, leading to many different mistakes in a child's upbringing. The essence of discipline is training children to act according to what you expect from them. Take time to talk to your child and make them know that you listen to them. They will learn to develop empathy when they understand that everyone has feelings. By teaching them kindness, you will give them the tools to understand why rules are essential to minimize conflict at home, school, and outside.

How do you discipline your child? Discipline is a style rather than a tool to be used, and it should not be punitive. It is finding the best approach at just the right moment. This parent-tested, research-based approach will help you understand why children act the way they do and give you specific tools that are positive instead of negative. Discipline and parenting education help you create a positive connection with your child, instill boundaries, teach new skills, and model behaviors. Using discipline is an opportunity to nurture your child's development by guiding, encouraging, and supporting them rather than simply reacting.

Gentle Discipline

You have the power to change lives simply by changing your style of discipline. It comes naturally to many parents to try "gentle discipline."[96-97] Gentle discipline is about educating children using positive reinforcement and encouragement. This style of discipline and love go hand in hand. Gentle discipline is about creating guidelines, boundaries, and expectations for your children, and these tools teach life lessons that help them thrive in their future. This collaborative parenting style of discipline is a respectful and peaceful approach to redirecting your child to follow social norms. The gentle discipline relies on a parenting philosophy, which focuses on training parents to tune with their child's developmental needs and respecting them as independent humans with good perspectives and feelings that deserve to be heard and honored.

If gentle discipline implies love, it could be essential in raising your child. A good parent can make a child feel the consequences of wrong behavior but never damages the bond that they share. Simple yet effective strategies will help you achieve this. Discipline is one of the most challenging parts of parenting. But you don't have to scream, spank or threaten your child to get him to obey you. Choose a discipline style that you feel good about and will use consistently. As you work gently to discipline your child, remember that learning requires positive and negative feedback. Your most important job is to give your child love and security, so he'll learn to trust you.

Discipline in rearing your preschooler is both necessary and very challenging. In the words of Theodor Seuss Geisel,[98] the famous

American children's author, who penned his works as Dr. Seuss: "Children want the same things we want. To laugh, be challenged, be entertained, and be delighted."[99] How do we provide what our children need in a manner that will not harm them or damage their self-esteem? Gently guide children to make the right decisions and understand and be aware of their behavior. However, discipline is not merely a tool for influencing behavior; it is a way of understanding and parenting our children. A child's personality takes form by the warmth we provide for them, the playtime, and the attention. These values include what we instill in them, the songs we teach them, and even our speech during parenting. Give your child a head start to the best possible future by keeping them intelligent, happy, and creative through our extensive parenting support and gentle discipline.

Boundary-Based Discipline

The Boundary-Based discipline[100] is a simple and easy-to-use style of discipline. This style is respectful and practical. It has been used by countless parents and professionals worldwide, but at its core, it boils down to two principles: First, establish boundaries and, Second, hold your child accountable. This style of discipline is what it sounds like. The parent sets clear limits and consequences to teach the child appropriate behavior and facilitate effective communication. The Boundary-Based approach does not allow for negotiation or warnings and does not allow for excessive consequences but does allow reteaching.

Thus, Boundary-Based Discipline is a fancy way to say rules with no gray area: If you do this, this is what happens. This style of discipline leads to more curiosity and less confusion for children. Boundary-Based discipline creates a clear picture of how the world works, from how much television you can watch on a school night to what will happen if you hit your sister. Boundary-Based discipline means keeping your children safe and healthy, teaching them to be responsible for their actions, and having them do their part in the family. Just like boundaries in other areas of life, parental boundaries instill security by giving children the freedom to explore. Boundaries help children know what we expect from them; then, it is much easier to correct misbehavior because it violates a clear rule when they mess up. Boundary-Based discipline leads to happier children and stronger relationships with the adults in their lives.

"Authoritative" Discipline

"Authoritative" Discipline[101] can help you guide your child without over-controlling or allowing too much freedom. By understanding and respecting each other, the bond between parent and child becomes even more robust. You take the guesswork away from parenting by enforcing and reinforcing clear limits and logical consequences. Your actions, responses, and facial expressions will be consistent, reassuring your children and letting them know that you have their best interests. A study from 1999 by Anne C. Fletcher and Brandi C. Jefferies suggested that having at least one authoritative parent can make a big difference regarding adolescent substance use.[102]

"Authoritative" Discipline allows for a loving response when a minor mishap, such as a spill on the kitchen floor. It takes a strong sense of boundaries to be parents, and we need to learn how to place them appropriately and guard them vigilantly. I believe that everything you do in this world has consequences. Obey the signs and speed limits on a road, and you'll avoid getting ticketed by the police. Eat too many sweets, and you'll probably get a stomachache from all that sugar. Discipline your child to make good decisions, and they will learn to make good decisions on their own when they get older.

Emotion Coaching

Different types of discipline are like other types of food: they all can be good in their way. The Emotion Coaching [103-104] style of discipline is like fast food: it can provide quick energy. This discipline isn't about punishment; it's about establishing a lasting relationship that teaches your child to behave responsibly. This relationship means understanding the reasons behind your child's misbehavior which is where emotional coaching comes in. Here's how it works: when you see your child struggling or upset, offer them empathy and help them identify the emotion they're feeling. Expressions such as "You feel sad because you didn't get what you wanted" or "It hurts when I say no" can help your child understand their feelings. Once they're able to recognize and label their emotions, then problem-solving around the negative behavior can begin.

Try emotion coaching to teach children internal self-regulation, which can establish healthy patterns that support behavior over the long term. The type of discipline used has the power to affect a child's self-esteem, hormone regulation, and ability to self-regulate. Research shows that empathy is a crucial ingredient for optimal development. Empathy is an emotion that triggers other emotions, and it can be a powerful driver of positive social behaviors. In fact, empathy predicts prosocial behaviors across many domains.[105] Emotion coaching lays down this foundation of effective discipline by teaching children to solve problems with guidance from an adult. It is natural for children to receive discipline as they grow and mature. Discipline encourages good habits and teaches them what is acceptable in society and what is not. We should not disparage any helpful techniques applied in the appropriate context. Time-outs have their place, as do "the look" and other ways parents choose to discipline their children.

When empathetic, positive responses to children are consistent and frequent, children learn to be emotionally competent. In contrast, approaches that do not focus on feelings or punish negative emotions can reinforce emotional problems. As a result, self-consciousness, chronic anxiety, depression, or even non-compliance are likely to occur. Parenting is all about striking a balance. Structure and discipline affect kids' stress levels and teach them how to lead balanced lives—even when life is not precisely "balanced," their sense of structure can be. But complementing your child's developmental needs with practical and consistent discipline is essential.

How to Discipline

Good discipline is fair, kind, consistent, and constructive. Discipline helps children feel secure because they come to trust that they will do what you say you're going to do. Here are some more essential benefits of discipline. A high score in the "discipline pillar" means your child is a person who is trained to be responsible, productive, and capable of achieving essential goals as an adult. Consistent discipline is the best way to teach a child that actions have consequences. To ensure that your child grows up to be a responsible adult, it is crucial that you set boundaries and apply some form of discipline when they don't help around the house or do their homework. Consistency in this area will teach them responsibility and respect for other people's space and time.

Set Realistic Expectations

Parenting is never easy. There's a reason why there are parenting experts, and it's hard to find one who doesn't claim to be an expert. When you begin parenting, you may have high expectations of your child, but they might not be as realistic as they could be. However, realistic expectations are essential when it comes to disciplining your child. They keep you from overreacting in situations that seem like misbehavior but are just natural development. You shouldn't expect your child to be perfect. You can't expect them never to cry or get into things they shouldn't. The truth is that up until two years old or so, babies will cry some of the time. This stage will pass once they learn how important it is for you to know that they need something—food or attention—or when they realize that the only way out of a situation is to stop crying. On the other side, teenagers' independence will remind us to establish realistic expectations.

Reinforce Good Behavior

Take advantage of good behavior and reinforce it! Good behavior is a virtue, and it deserves praise. Pat on the back, hugs, and smiles will work wonders when reinforcing good behavior in your child. No matter how hard we try, our children cannot avoid making mistakes. They will act out, speak inappropriately, and disobey us at times. If a discipline episode arises, we need to choose an appropriate consequence and follow through. However, it's also essential for us to reinforce good behavior by praising our children in an encouraging way when they behave well. In other words, stay positive no matter what! Say things like, "It was nice that you did that!" and "I love it when you help your sister," or "Because you behaved so well today, let's play the extra game tonight." When we reward children, it is more likely that they will behave well.

A positive reinforcement strategy is at the heart of positive parenting. Reinforce good behavior by giving your child praise and attention when they do something right. You are setting the table, and your daughter puts her napkin on her lap without being told to do so; now would be the perfect time to compliment her and give her a high five for doing a good job. This same principle can also be applied when children show bad or harmful behavior. However, it may be tempting to give them negative feedback when they do not follow directions while cleaning their room or behave aggressively towards other children; instead, you remain calm and ignore their actions. The goal is to raise kind, responsible children who will eventually become kind, responsible adults.

Be Aware of Your Own Needs and Reactions

Most parents can agree that raising a child is no small task. It's a full-time job that requires long hours alternating between tough love and encouraging gentle guidance. As a parent, you will have days when you feel like you have no control. Sometimes parents need a time-out themselves. If you feel upset, make sure to take some time to cool down. If a child acts up at the grocery store, do you feel intimidated? If your tween seems moody, do you think they need an attitude adjustment? Do you cringe with embarrassment at how your teen reacted when her curfew lasted for another night? "Discipline" didn't just happen overnight. It evolves as we mature and grow into our roles as parents.

Discipline is something you give yourself and something you must have if you hope to become the best person you can be. It's born of maturity, facing life with an even gaze, and making wise decisions. Self-discipline empowers you to live for a larger purpose instead of becoming a serf to your fears. Parenting is never an easy task, some days it can be rewarding, and on others, it can be frustrating. Sometimes the best way to understand your children better is to look in the mirror. In discipline be aware of your own needs and reactions; you will learn how to recognize your emotions, control them so you can discipline effectively, change damaging behaviors, avoid power struggles and manage stress levels. The beauty of parenting is that there's no handbook to follow. You're making it up as you go along. This book has one main goal: helping you improve your relationship with your children, so they become healthy, happy adults. A wholesome and proper upbringing prepares your child to face the World independently and confidently.

FREEDOM

"Bodily exercise, when compulsory, does no harm to the body; but knowledge which is acquired under compulsion obtains no hold on the mind."
—Plato, The Republic [15]

We all desire the freedom to be whoever we want to be. But did you realize that you can nurture this freedom in your children as a parent? Childhood is a particular time of life. It is the period when we learn, explore and develop into adults. The freedom to pursue dreams is necessary to crave fulfillment in adulthood. A child deprived of sight and hearing would still be intelligent and able to learn. Children are naturally gifted, but their environment often stifles their talents. When you have a child with special needs, be careful not to expect too much of them. Freedom and love, and discipline are essential in a child's education. A flexible approach, one that encourages children to express their individuality, is key to a child's learning. Giving children simple choices from an early age can be beneficial. If you provide them with a choice between two or three items or between two things they want to do, it can help them determine what they prefer and why that choice appeals to them. Choice opportunities encourage them to exercise their free will, which helps develop their self-confidence.

Freedom is at the core of what it means to be human. Without freedom, people cannot fulfill their potential and reach their goals. Independence is important because it makes it possible for people to learn, develop and pursue happiness. Freedom and discipline working together encourage children to feel in control, which leads them to create healthy self-esteem. It also helps them become independent thinkers who can make more informed decisions about their lives, especially after leaving school. When children have responsibility and freedom within boundaries, they learn that mistakes are part of life, and it's essential to learn from them to do better next time. Independence also creates an open-minded attitude that encourages critical thinking, which is vital as we grow older and become aware of the world around us. Freedom taught at an early age helps children grow into well-rounded individuals who can be productive members of society. Without this crucial ingredient, a child's learning, growth, or development are unnecessarily limited. Children need to learn through their experiences and their mistakes. One day, they will become independent individuals who could build a better world for us all.

Understanding Freedom

Freedom is a word we use a lot in our lives—and often misunderstood. We hear it all the time, but what does it mean? What does it mean to be free? In this book, we'll discuss two kinds of freedom: First, "freedom from," also known as freedom of indifference." And second, "freedom for excellence." We parents need to grasp the difference between the freedom that focuses on being able to choose and freedom that seeks something with enduring goodness and value.

For most of us, freedom is the ability to make our own decisions without the constraint of others or coercion. However, this is an incomplete understanding of freedom. This kind of freedom—freedom of indifference—is the view that characterizes much of our culture. In the modern World, freedom centers on individual autonomy. According to this view, discipline is always a problem. It is something accepted or done as a sort of necessary evil. In simple words, this type of freedom is freedom without intrinsic relation to the purpose. It does not foster discipline; it somewhat undermines it. Pursuing virtue, goodness, and responsibility is not integral to this "freedom." In this case, we make choices without considering any ultimate goals. It is as if there was nothing to gain from virtue. It would be like giving our children the possibility of choosing without regard for their character or understanding of reality. If this concept of freedom has shaped us as parents, we could inadvertently pass it on to our children. This kind of freedom in the hands of a child can be a double-edged sword that could hurt them instead of helping them.

Freedom for Excellence

Freedom for excellence is a powerful concept that helps men and women become what they can be. Throughout history, great teachers and thinkers have understood this idea, which has been so important to Western Civilization. In other words, freedom for excellence is the freedom that sees discipline as a tool for a higher level of freedom. Cultivating a garden, creating art, working on a project, starting a business, and learning a new language are all examples of activities that follow this pattern—you get out what you put into them. For example, if you want to learn another language, then through discipline, you must put in the time and effort necessary to do so. Then you can enjoy the freedom of speaking a language fluently. Servais Theodore Pinckaers,[106] a Belgian noted moral theologian and Roman Catholic priest, is an author who talks about this concept and uses the metaphor of playing a musical instrument well to illustrate it. Only someone who has practiced a piece many times has the freedom to play it well in concert. The same applies to people who achieve goals in all different areas in life. You will find the combination of discipline, talent, learning, and practice preceding freedom.

Theologians and philosophers have linked this type of freedom to concepts like discipline, purpose, goodness, the actualization of possibilities, and virtue. Robert Baron—an American Roman Catholic Bishop, media personality, author, and theologian—encapsulated this concept in one phrase: "Freedom for excellence is the shaping of desire so as to make the achievement of the good first possible and then effortless."[107] In other words, it is a path from which we can realize our highest aspirations by taking advantage of what nature has given us. We are free only when we can freely discipline our lives so that what might seem almost impossible becomes a reality. In a child's education, freedom is not about what they want to do but what they can do. A child learns to recognize that there are things they can do and other things that they cannot do. Also, "I can do what I want" is not the same as "I can do what I ought." The first takes nothing seriously; the second takes everything seriously— even him or herself. Teach your children a kind of freedom that is, ultimately, not the right to do what they want but the ability to do what they ought. With this in mind, having room for choice will not be confused with license. We should instruct our children about fundamental things that are good, right, and necessary in their lives.

Teach your child that to become great at doing something, they first need to learn and then practice until they can do it effortlessly with joy, freedom, and newfound creativity. The more the game's moves become yours, the freer you become in playing baseball through exercise and discipline. Then when you become able to play effortlessly and with excellence, you can do what the game demands of you within the rules of the game. For the freedom of indifference, objective rules, orders, and disciplines are not aid but a problem, for they are felt only as limitations. But for the second type of freedom, such laws are liberating, for they make the achievement of some great good possible. In a world where we restrain children more, partly for safety concerns, our approach to children's education should be freeing. We want children to successfully navigate the challenges of adulthood by giving them the tools to make not just any choices but wise choices. Love, discipline, and teach your child aiming at freedom for excellence. Let them explore their interests and watch them flourish, not just in school but in life.

What is Free Play?

Play is free, so there's no excuse for not making time for it. And play is an essential ingredient in any child's recipe for success. Free play is beneficial and essential for children.[108-112] The American Academy of Pediatrics made recommendations to pediatricians regarding free play:

"Pediatricians can promote free play as a healthy, essential part of childhood. They should recommend that all children are afforded ample, unscheduled, independent, nonscreen time to be creative, to reflect, and to decompress. They should emphasize that although parents can certainly monitor play for safety, a large proportion of play should be child driven rather than adult directed."[113]

The American Academy of Pediatrics discovered some exciting benefits, including:

1. Free play allows children to use their creativity and develop their imagination and other strengths.

2. Encourages children to interact with and explore the world around them.

3. It helps children adjust to school and enhance their learning readiness, behavior, and problem-solving skills.

4. It helps children learn and practice self-regulation.

5. It helps children build decision-making skills.

It's all about having fun. Playful games like hide and seek boost your child's cognitive function. Make sure your little one has plenty of opportunity for free play so they can develop essential skills for later life!

Play is one of the primary forms of human expression and development. Children play because they want to, not because they have to. Play is a big part of childhood, and it can come in many different forms. Some children like to be active and use their imaginations with dramatic play, while others prefer quieter activities like building with blocks or drawing. Each type of play has its benefits, but it's essential not to take away a child's freedom to choose how they play. Children will still learn valuable things even if it looks like they're just being silly. Children learn best by having fun. Children are natural learners in the right conditions, and freedom to play is an integral part of that picture. It's also why we need to make sure that children have the time, space, support, and encouragement they need to do what comes naturally:

- Explore, experiment, and expand their senses.
- Try new things.
- Work out who they are.
- Create something from nothing.
- Be children and have fun while learning.

With the freedom to explore, play, and imagine, children better understand the world around them. This freedom helps prepare children for school and enhances their learning readiness, behavior, and problem-solving skills. But it's not just the freedom to play that produces these benefits; it is also how children play and what they use to play. As you prepare to send your children (or grandchild) off to school, let's take a quick look at what defines free play and what makes it so important.

Unstructured play is an essential part of childhood development, and it's a category of play in which children engage in open-ended play with no specific learning objective. It can also be called "free play," and many would say that it is "letting kids be kids." That's it. It's just a bunch of kids playing without any adults telling them what to do or how. When adults leave children alone to their imaginations, they're likely to get up in front of a group and sing, dance, and act silly. They might also run around wildly and wrestle with each other. Children might use props like sticks or hula hoops or build forts out of blankets and chairs. Some will even sit there quietly by themselves, reading a book! The point is that free play gives kids room to learn many skills through exploring and experimenting in different ways.

The magic of free play is that it's all about playing, not just performing. Instead of being goal-oriented, the focus is on a process, like "pretend play" or "shared storytelling." Free play is fun. The kind of fun that can make a child's day. The type of fun makes your heart swell with joy when you see them genuinely having a good time. It is the kind of fun that captures the essence of childhood and helps shape it into adulthood. Let your kids be kids. There is no limit to how much fun they can have if allowed to play unsupervised, especially with four or more friends. Even better, they will learn the social skills to grow and thrive in a group.

Free play is free. To put it this way: it comes with the price of admission. It's called free play for a reason—if your children yearn to create their own stories and characters, let them, and if they want to sit quietly and put together Legos, great! If they're going to build an elaborate city out of blocks or act out a pirate adventure, that's cool. Free play is just that—free. The difference between unstructured play and structured play is the ultimate intent. Unstructured play is unplanned and often spontaneous, with no particular rules to follow. Sometimes it's inspired by the materials at hand and other kids' ideas.

In summary, free play is a play that parents do not structure. It's a child-directed activity where the child chooses what they want to do and how they wish. Free play can occur wherever your child feels comfortable—in their bedroom, in the den, outside the backyard, or with other children. Of course, sometimes it's helpful for them to participate in structured activities like music classes or soccer practice. One thing about these activities is that though there are rules for them (such as a time limit for soccer practice), adults don't try to make decisions for the children taking part in them.

Ideas to Facilitate Free Play

Supervised free play is essential to a preschooler's physical and social development. Encourage your child's creativity by providing a variety of safe, age-appropriate toys and materials for unstructured playtime. Sit back and relax; help children get the most out of unstructured playtime. Set up toys, with enough space, and plenty of time. And don't forget the nontraditional items! Play can be a lot of fun, but it helps to have the right equipment. Some nontraditional things are perfect for encouraging preschoolers to engage in unstructured play: balls of different sizes, cardboard boxes, paper towel rolls, blocks, sidewalk chalk, or simply sticks and rocks. Sometimes kids want to play. They don't need any equipment or even a game plan—they just want to get down on the floor and do whatever they feel like doing.

One Word about Structured Play

Structured play [114,115] is when you set specific goals for your child, and they get to try to achieve them, either by themselves or with the help of a trusted adult. Most children like to play, but it can be hard to stay focused. Structured play helps your child learn specific life skills at home and develop critical physical abilities and gives your child a chance to have fun while learning. Parents and teachers can help kids by creating simple games that use everyday items found around the house. Children may work on essential life skills like understanding the months of the year or basic physical skills such as throwing a ball and hitting a target. Kids can do structured play all by themselves or with friends!

Thus, structured play is not always just an organized activity. Sometimes, it can be as simple as teaching your child how to throw a ball into a laundry basket or giving them directions to follow, such as "Simon says." By teaching your preschooler how to throw a ball into a laundry basket, you provide them with a framework for their activity. Another example of structured play would be enrolling your child in music lessons or soccer practice; structured activities can have many benefits even when they don't seem "educational." Structured play is any activity with rules and regulations on how to play. Activities such as board games and organized sports are examples of structured play. Other types of structured play include puzzles, traditional games play by children based on simple rules, and classes your child may have already tried.

Structured play complements free play in the learning experience of your children. This kind of play helps shape their motor skills, creativity, and sportsmanship. We have already addressed concerns that structured play may not allow children to cultivate as much of their self-initiated creativity by advocating both free and structured play. Many educational advocates argue that a lot of free play can occur within a certain degree of structure. Teach your child the foundation for a strong future by providing structured play activities. Getting your kids to play is a serious business – make the most of this beautiful tool to help your child grow, be happy, and healthy!

Physical Activity

You might say we're raising a generation of couch potatoes. Children who spend their days in front of screens and cars may be missing out on crucial brain-building opportunities. Physical activity is an essential part of young children's lives, but too many get less than the recommended one hour of physical activity per day. In obesity and overweight children, we have a severe problem. And while a child's diet may be the starting point, what they are doing physically throughout their day is just as important. Children need at least 60 minutes of physical activity each day[116]—ideally more—for good health and to avoid weight gain. But an estimated 43 million preschool children worldwide were overweight or obese in 2010—an increase of 60 percent since 1990.[117] This situation has only worsened during the past decade. Leading scientists from around the globe found physical activity declines as much as 40 percent between ages 2 and 5 years old. In the United States, The White House Task Force on Childhood Obesity[118] founded by the Obama Administration on February 9, 2010, reported that over half of obese children become overweight by age two, while one in five children are obese by the time they turn six.

Following the ancient principle of "mens sana in corpore sano," or a sound mind in a sound body, regular physical exercise can reduce stress and anxiety, improve sleep quality, and help you lose weight and gain muscle.[119-122] Play is an exercise for the brain, and it can benefit children in so many ways: it helps them develop gross motor skills and fine motor skills, promotes creativity and problem solving, and can even help build social skills! And the best part? Playing doesn't have to be expensive or complicated! Children can play anywhere, safe—indoors or outdoors; alone or with other children; with toys or without toys; during scheduled time slots, or whenever they feel like it. Help your child stay healthy and active! Research shows that toddlers learn many of their lifelong movement patterns when playing with their peers. An organized playtime helps them to develop socially, physically, and cognitively. Active children are likely to do better in school, develop a healthy body image, and be more motivated to participate in daily physical activity.

When you're a child, it's all about play—and that's a good thing! Parents know that play is vital for their kids' development, but they may not realize how much it can help. Let's look at some of the ways playing helps children learn:

— Play helps children learn to problem solve. When kids play games, they must think through what they need to do next to succeed at the game, and this can help them develop strategies and skills that they can use later on in life.

— Play helps children learn to negotiate and share. When kids play together, they need to determine who gets which toy or who goes next according to the rules, etc. They'll also need to figure out how many people can play with one toy at a time—and whether everyone needs permission before taking something from another child.

— Play can help children develop and maintain friendships. When two or more kids play together, they might create rules for their game (like how many points you get for hitting someone else with an imaginary sword). These rules help them coordinate their actions and stay focused on what everyone wants from the game, so everyone has fun!

Role-playing Games

Have you ever thought about the benefits of role-playing games for children? Role-playing games[123,124] are a fantastic way to foster creativity and imagination in your children. They can help your child develop social skills, learn how to problem solve, and improve their communication ability. Some examples of role-playing games include make-believe, playing house, or pretending to be a teacher or doctor. For example, the American Academy of Pediatrics states that "role play can help children learn about emotions and empathy."[112] Children who engage in role-playing games tend to be more empathetic than those who don't participate in such activities. They may also have an easier understanding of what other people feel when they're upset or angry (rather than just reacting negatively).

It helps children practice communication skills without being judged by peers if they say something wrong or make a mistake because it is a game, but it also gives parents and teachers a way to help their children in a fun environment! Role-playing games are an excellent way for kids to practice social skills and develop critical thinking. They can also help children develop a sense of responsibility and self-control. Here's how:

1. Make-believe games help kids learn to be flexible with their imaginations and use their creativity.

2. Playing house teaches them how to work within a group toward a common goal.

3. Pretending to be a parent or other adult allows them to practice taking on adult roles—and helps them get used to being an adult someday!

4. Climbing trees, playing in the mud, and other outdoor activities promote physical activity in fun and engaging ways for kids, so they'll want to do more!

5. Learn how to solve problems by themselves, without always relying on someone else for help.

6. They learn to get comfortable with trying new things and taking risks.

7. They develop their social skills, such as talking to others, sharing information, and listening carefully.

8. Children learn how to work together with friends

Choice Within Certain Limits

When you're a parent, it's easy to feel like your job is to give your child a million rules and regulations. But what if I told you that giving your children more freedom could make them happier and healthier? That's right—a recent study found that giving kids more autonomy can improve the well-being of everyone in the family. The study from the Child Development journal—and according to Psychology Today[125]—found that families who gave children more freedom were associated with improved well-being for everyone—parents and children alike—during the pandemic. Parents who gave their children more autonomy discovered they did better emotionally. Freedom within limits provided benefits, including a greater sense of fulfillment and a more emotionally bonded family. Parenting involving "choice within certain limits seemed to be optimal," the researchers concluded.

As a parent, you want your children to feel safe and secure. But how do you ensure that they are safe while encouraging them to explore the world around them? By allowing your children room for exploration, they will learn to trust themselves and trust others more quickly than when they are on a very tight leash throughout their childhoods. By allowing them room for exploration without fear or guilt on your part, you will also demonstrate that it is okay for people—even young ones—to make mistakes or fail at times. Here's an opportunity to encourage them to try hard enough next time!

Creating a Sense of Security

Early in your children's lives, safety is paramount. You want to create a sense of security in your child. First, they need to learn that you are a safe harbor they can always return to and find protection when required. Then, by allowing them time and space for exploration, you show that you trust them—and this builds confidence for years down the road! These two steps can be challenging: often, when we try to protect our children from unpleasant experiences, we unintentionally stunt their development by denying them growth opportunities. It's so important that we give our children room to make mistakes and learn from them—and it's even more critical that we don't overreact when they make mistakes! Cultivate your sense of confidence that this is possible without endangering your child's safety. If your child is doing something dangerous or harmful (e.g., playing with matches), act by removing them from the situation immediately. Do not ignore or cover up their behavior—make sure your children know what behavior is unacceptable so that they don't repeat it!

Children are like little sponges. They soak up everything around them. If you want to raise a confident and independent child, you'll need to help them find their confidence by giving them space for exploration. You want your child to feel confident in his ability to explore the world around them and take on challenges head-on. You don't want them to feel like they can't handle things on their own or need someone else's help if something goes wrong. It's essential for them not just because it teaches them about life but because it helps them develop self-confidence that will serve them well throughout life. When your children are young and dependent on you for protection and comfort, take the opportunity to build a sense of security in them. It's hard to learn new skills and push ourselves out of our comfort zones if we never feel safe and secure. That's why it's essential to build our kids' confidence from the inside out so they're ready to take on challenges and explore their potential. By encouraging our children to try new things and learn from their mistakes, we're helping them find competence, self-respect, and independence within themselves.

If you want your kids to be independent, then make them! I'm serious—if you want your kids to be able to take care of themselves and make good decisions, then let them do it. You don't need to micromanage their lives or control every aspect. Allowing them space for exploration will enable them to experience life fully, learn important lessons about themselves and the world around them, and develop the skills they need to be successful later in life.

How Do I Know If I Am Raising Independent Children?

Being independent is a beautiful trait to have. It means that you can take care of yourself and know how to do things on your own. You are confident in your abilities, and you know what it takes to get things done. By letting your children explore on their terms, you give them the skills they need to succeed in life—and that's something everyone wants. Then, how do I know if I am raising independent children? Look for the following characteristics and use them as guidelines as you educate your child:

— You and your children are not in a controlling relationship but in one that encourages collaboration and expressing ideas and opinions. Independent children have high emotional maturity, empathy, trustworthiness, and concern for others' needs in relationships with family members and friends. The child will tend to have a sense of humor about life's difficulties; they will laugh at their own mistakes rather than get angry or upset. Independent Children are also great collaborators who enjoy working with other people and talking with them about ideas and plans.

· FREEDOM ·

— Their motivation comes from within rather than imposed by parents or other adults because they are allowed to find their reasons to do things and set and accomplish goals. With independence comes a healthy sense of self. They can make decisions independently, with minimal input from other people. They can set and achieve goals for themselves with the help of others when needed.

— Independent children are independent problem solvers. Even though they may ask for help occasionally, it's because they want guidance from an expert rather than because they need someone else to solve their problems.

— Finally, parents who reinforce good child behavior by using extrinsic rewards appropriately and in limited proportion tend to have more independent children. When parents collaborate with their children in making decisions about what to do together, it helps build a sense of shared responsibility that leads to more independence. And when parents solicit their children's ideas and wishes, they help them develop self-confidence and initiative. A child's decisions tend to come more from him or herself than from outside.

Have you not noticed how your kids are always trying to do everything themselves? They want to make their lunches, take care of their pets and even clean up after themselves. Well, that's not all they can do! They're also excellent listeners who hear what you have to say (if you ask them nicely). Independent children are a good help because they can do all kinds of stuff without your assistance. So, if you want your kids to grow up knowing how to handle themselves in the World, follow these simple tips:

• Use extrinsic rewards sparingly.

• Ask your children for their opinion before making important decisions (like what school they should go to).

• Please encourage your children's independence by giving them tasks that will help develop their skills (like setting the table or cleaning their room).

Some parents can go too far when it comes to external rewards, and sometimes, it's downright harmful. Here are some examples of when the use of extrinsic rewards goes from helping your child learn independence to hurting them:

* When a parent insists on paying for things for their child instead of letting them buy them themselves (or paying for something without asking first).

* When a parent constantly gives their child money in exchange for chores around the house, instead of encouraging them to do it because they want to be helpful.

* When a parent gives their child an allowance instead of encouraging them to save up their spending money themselves.

If you find yourself falling into any of these traps, don't worry! You now understand how to achieve a balanced approach to improve your relationship with your children to feel more independent while still maintaining structure and boundaries in their lives.

Freedom and Responsibility

As a parent, you are responsible for providing your children the opportunities to be independent. But for them to be truly independent, they must take advantage of those opportunities and do what is necessary to maximize them. Your child needs to be responsible and disciplined and involved in helping with chores around the house. They should take care of their belongings by keeping them neat and clean. They should also take care of their schoolwork by doing it on time without needing to be reminded too often. Your children should also keep their rooms clean. It looks nice when guests come over or when family members visit you at home during holidays or other special occasions such as birthdays or anniversaries. Your children need to stay committed means that they need to follow through with your plans regarding homework assignments or other responsibilities at school or home (such as chores). Combining freedom and responsibility means that your child should be able to make good choices about how much time to spend on activities outside of schoolwork (such as playing video games), sports practices (such as soccer practice), socializing, and other activities.

In a sense, you can't teach independence. But it can become a gift from you to your child. If you're a parent, then you know this to be true. Your children are not born with the ability to be independent—they need your help. And that's okay! Independence is not something that your children can gain independently, and they have neither the experience nor the capacity to be autonomous without your cooperation. However, by being intentional about it, you can provide your child with an essential foundation for gaining independence.

Give Your Children Love and Respect

Children love to feel loved and respected by their parents. And while they may not like to admit it, they need their parent's respect. Our first chapter considered how essential this is for children's development. Your children need to feel loved and respected to build confidence in themself. If you cannot do this because of your issues or how you were raised, your child may never learn to be independent and become dependent for life. So, make sure that you love and respect yourself first!

If you have young children, your world has changed. You now have two beautiful little people who rely on you for all their physical and emotional needs. Children want to know that they can count on us; their security and self-esteem depend upon it. It's hard enough being a parent without having to deal with our issues. Whatever they are, let's do our best to resolve them as we start parenting! As a result, your children will be a gift wrapped in many other gifts, including maturity in every aspect of your life.

Show Confidence in Your Children's Capabilities

In the same manner, you might need to work on your self-confidence so you can share it with your child. Show confidence in your children's capabilities. Children need to feel capable of accomplishing things independently; otherwise, they will always seek out other people who will give them direction and help them make decisions—which means they won't be making decisions! So, show your children that they can accomplish many things—even if it seems overwhelming at first!

Independence Requires Self-Discipline

It is worth repeating! Teach discipline to your child. First, it comes from you but gradually, it becomes something the child owns. As grownups, we know it: independence requires self-discipline. Teach them that they have control over their lives. Freedom comes from feeling like one can develop control over one's thoughts and actions, primarily when oriented towards what is good, right, and worthy of being pursued. But have you ever tried to teach your kids about responsibility? It's hard. Kids are, well, kids. They don't always understand what it means to be responsible for themselves or others. But that doesn't mean you can't teach them!

Self-Discipline Requires Responsibility

One of the best ways to ensure that your children succeed is to teach them responsibility. The more they feel like they have control over their own lives, the more empowered they will be to make choices that improve themselves and their environment. Here are some tips for helping your children become more responsible:

1) Make a list with your children of their responsibilities. Next, identify others who will have responsibilities (and what they are) in your children's achievement activities, such as teachers, instructors, or coaches. This list includes you! It might seem overkill at first, but it's essential to make sure everyone is on the same page regarding responsibilities and consequences so that no one seems like they're getting away with something—or worse!—getting punished unfairly.

2) Once everyone knows their roles and responsibilities, assign consequences for not fulfilling those roles and responsibilities. Make a list of what you as a parent will be doing to help your children succeed.

3) There should also be consequences for not fulfilling responsibilities. Consequences could include removing something of importance to your children and giving them the control to get it back by acting appropriately—for example, losing computer privileges or not being allowed out at night. This process clarifies for both you and your children your "jobs" and helps keep everyone on the same page when someone is missing out!

A Three Cord Rope

In the Hebrew Scriptures, "a three-cord rope"[126] refers to a cord of three braided strands intertwined together. This type of cord is tough to break. What gives strength to the rope is the unity of the three strands. Our strong rope needs to have three strands braided together: Love, Discipline, and Freedom. These interwoven strands will have a solid and durable vitality in your child's life. What a great metaphor this is for how this dynamic should work. You can't have one without the other two. Love is the first strand in our cord of three. Without love, there would be nothing else but chaos in our lives and relationships lacking the glue to keep the strands united and the rope of our lives strong.

Discipline is the second strand in our cord of three. We need to learn how to discipline ourselves to live a life pleasing to God rather than pleasing ourselves as individuals without discipline. Even if you don't believe in God, we all need a higher ideal to sustain and inspire our lives. Freedom is the third strand in our cord of three. Freedom means making choices for ourselves without feeling like someone else controls us or dictates what we do. As we have seen already, this also means pursuing what is good and excellent with our decisions. If you love someone with no discipline or freedom, it will be challenging to get them to do what you want them to do. If you want your children to behave, they need some freedom and discipline from their parents. If you want your employees to work hard and perform well at work, they need some discipline and freedom from their managers or employers. Whether personal or professional, no matter what kind of relationship you're in, these three elements are always present in some form or another, whether explicit or implicit, obvious or subtle. Now, let's move on to the material that will cover our rope for additional strength and protection: Instruction. Wait, instruction is part of this book "as a whole." Teaching our kids love, discipline, and independence is an instruction of the most valuable quality. In any case, let's look now at instruction itself.

INSTRUCTION

"Train a child in the way appropriate for him, and when he becomes older, he will not turn from it."
—*Proverbs 22:6,126*

Secrets Of Your Child's Brain

The brain is a beautiful organ, and your child's brain is amazing. Scientists marvel at how wonderfully and mysteriously it develops. The early postnatal period is one of the most active periods in a baby's brain development, characterized by dramatic changes from physical structure to cognition. A child's brain increases in size by four-fold during the preschool period, and it reaches about 90% of adult volume by age 6.[127,128] During this time, babies start to say their first words and express themselves via gestures and facial expressions. During the first two years of life, connections form between neurons, and synapses develop quickly. But structural changes in both the major gray and white matter brain structures continue through childhood and adolescence—these changes parallel changes in the functional organization that manifest in behavior.

Babies are awesome. They are so young and fragile, but somehow, they manage to get through their first few years of life. We may always wonder how they manage to do it, but science has shed some light on how babies' brains are more connected than adult brains. In fact, during the early period after your child's birth, the number of connections throughout the developing brain far exceeds that of adults. Plasticity allows young infants to learn rapidly and adapt to their environment. Early childhood brain development is the extraordinary process by which neurons grow and make connections. Then, this exuberant connectivity gradually subsides due to pruning via processes connected to the child's experience. This early experience-dependent shaping of the young brain relies on neuroplasticity, a display of astonishing capacity for adaptation in preparation for life. This vitality is the hallmark of early brain development. With a high level of brain connectivity in early development, the child can better adapt and learn quickly. Like other organs in the body, brain development occurs both before and after birth. Your child's brain is continually growing, from forming cognitive abilities to improving motor skills.

The juvenile brain has a unique capacity for physical and functional change, as well as for adaptation. The temporal patterning of this magnificent process is the critical maturational period, where refinement of cellular connections occurs when the circuitry responds to environmental cues or threats. These experiences can be visual or auditory, tactile or sensory-based for the most part — they are all integrated by the developing organism. The effects of early experience on brain synaptic organization last into adulthood, creating the foundation that allows us to adapt to new challenges and demands. There is a greater level of connectivity during early childhood development than at any other time in life. We must invest early to protect and promote individual success throughout life.

Ready to Learn!

Children are born curious, interested, and ready to learn — but when does your child's brain start learning? As early as birth, a child is already learning. Every day, your child is continuously gaining new knowledge about their world. This experience will shape how they think about themselves and other people and how they interact with their surroundings. The first years of life are crucial to your child's development. They need to start learning as soon as possible! As soon as you meet your newborn baby, you can play with them, talk to them, and sing. Touch person-to-person contact is critical at this stage. Early childhood is a crucial period of brain development. During this early period, it bears repeating that the brain increases significantly in size mainly due to a rapid increase in the number of synaptic connections—those little gaps between neurons where information travels—particularly in the cerebral cortex. The hippocampus—a critical structure in the brain for memory and learning— also undergoes significant development parallel with other systems. The brain grows in quantity, four times its original size during early childhood, and quality. This massive increase is due mainly to an incredible surge in active synaptic connections.

Born with an Imitation Mechanism

Children learn through imitation. Time and time again, scientific studies prove it. Children learn through observation and then imitate the process or skill they observe. As kids, we often did this to mimic our parents and teachers to get their approval, but it became a way to express ourselves as individuals as we grew older. Do you remember the phrase "monkey see monkey do" from childhood? Children have a fantastic ability to observe what others do and then emulate it in their play. Whether they're watching Mom and Dad use a smartphone or a car, children will generally attempt to copy what they've seen. It's no wonder that many parents will be surprised when their child notices the bubbles their mother was busily forming on their wand and starts blowing them away with their own hands!

· INSTRUCTION ·

Children then imitate these actions to gain approval from an adult or older sibling—and perhaps get some candy along the way too!

Babies are so good at imitation that you can probably find them imitating you in the mirror now and then. That's because babies are hard-wired for imitation at birth. When they see people move, their brains try to make sense of what's going on and then store those movements as a memory. Psychologist Andrew Meltzoff [129-130]—a renowned researcher in this area—stuck his tongue out at 2- to 3-week-old babies. They did it back to him. Then he opened his mouth wide, pushed out his lips like a duck, and opened and closed the fingers of one hand. The babies did that too. In a very insightful and thought-provoking study on the emergence of imitation in human development, psychologist Andrew Meltzoff makes the case that imitation is not just copying. It's a form of communication between adults and children. (And it's also one way monkeys learn new things.) Andrew Meltzoff argues that imitation isn't simply an instinctive behavior but a sophisticated process we can teach infants. If you're having trouble getting your child to imitate you as much as you'd like them to, try this: don't ask them, "Do what I do" or even "Do what I say." Instead, say, "Let's do something together!" Then show them how something works—or doesn't—and help them figure out how they can do it themselves.

You learned how to tie your shoes by watching someone else do it, right? What do you do if you want to teach someone how to tie their shoes? You show them how. You demonstrate the motion of your hands, and then they learn it. And you learned to ride a bike by watching other people do it. You didn't have a handy manual that taught you how to do those things—you just watched and then practiced until you got it. The same is true for most things we know how to do as adults. We don't have any instruction manual or textbook that details exactly how each activity works; instead, we simply observe others doing those activities so that we can learn from them on an unconscious level.

We initially imitate when learning basic math skills, riding a bike, and tying shoes. It's only later in life (and sometimes not even then!) that we realize, "Hey! I learned this stuff without realizing it!". This method applies to skills like writing and speaking and purely mental ones (like reasoning). Our brains are pattern recognition machines, and humans learn by modeling their behavior after others. If you want your children to brush their teeth, parents don't need to tell them why their teeth will fall out if they don't. If you want children to stop hitting other kids, it's not strictly necessary for you to explain why aggression is wrong. They'll pick up on those lessons by watching what you do and listening to what you say—even if they can't articulate why certain behaviors are beneficial or harmful until much later in life.

Mirror neurons were discovered in the early 1990s by Italian neuroscientist Giacomo Rizzolatti.[131-132] He studied motor control in monkeys, trying to figure out what makes them move their hands and feet in synchrony with an object they were grasping (for example, when a monkey grabs a peanut). Dr. Rizzolatti found that some neurons in the brain would fire when a monkey caught something and when it watched another monkey do so. These cells seemed to have "mirror properties"—they would respond both to action and observation—and were therefore named "mirror neurons." You may have heard that we all have mirror neurons. When you see a person yawn, your mirror neurons are activated, and you start to yawn. Through these neuronal networks is how imitation happens—at least at the biological level—and it's a critical part of learning. This system seems to underpin imitative behaviors and is crucial in explaining how we understand others' minds and intentions and empathize with others' emotional states.

· INSTRUCTION ·

Imitation operates as a powerful tool in the proper context. It's the way we learn most of our behaviors, and you can use it to teach your kids—even those whose brains are still developing. After all, imitation itself is a form of learning—and it can be much more fun than just reading instructions or watching videos on YouTube. If you're looking for ways to teach your kids about safety or healthy eating habits, or anything else that involves social behavior, consider these tips:

• Show them how to do it by example. Your child will watch what you do more than listen to what you say!

• Do what needs doing now; don't wait until tomorrow when there might be time for another lesson plan (read: procrastination). Imitation isn't only crucial at an early age; it's also essential at any age!

You might have thought that imitation was only a bad thing, but the truth is that it's crucial to learning. We learn by imitating each other, whether we're imitating our parents or even our favorite stars. When children are discouraged from imitating, they can lose interest in school and develop a bad attitude toward learning, leading to later problems. They may not see the point of learning something if they don't see anyone else doing it. And because imitation plays such an essential role in your child's cognitive development, discouraging them from doing so could ultimately lead to low self-esteem issues and violent behavior (including bullying).

When discouraging imitation: Tell them why they shouldn't do something. When you tell your children "no" to something, you're only telling them not to do something at that moment. Tell them why they shouldn't do it if they imitate something dangerous, illegal, or immoral. You can help make the lesson stick better than simply saying "no," which doesn't give any specific reason other than what might happen if they did that without thinking first (such as getting in trouble).

Your Child Can Learn More Than You Think

New research shows that children's potential for learning is extraordinary.[133-136] They can learn many things before they can speak. These pre-linguistic cognitive skills serve as a foundation for future learning and development. When you hold your baby in your arms for the first time, it's hard to believe that an adorable little creature could be capable of learning. But babies have an extraordinary learning potential—and we're not just saying that because we're parents. It's true. Just think about everything babies learn in their first five years to prove it. They know how to make eye contact, shake hands, and wave "hello." They learn how to walk, talk and sing songs. They learn to understand what others are saying and what they mean when speaking. In short, they amaze us every day with all they have learned so far—and we haven't even touched on everything they know!

General stages of development do not necessarily limit children's cognitive development and learning. Historically, many people have identified development as progressing through several fixed stages and periods. However, researchers generally find that these developmental stages are more descriptive about the ability to demonstrate these skills rather than how the skills themselves transform through stages.

John Flavell, a prominent developmental psychologist, once noted that "as soon as one begins to talk about the nature of children's reasoning it becomes abundantly clear that the child's thinking is in fact sometimes advanced and sophisticated and hence not at all what one would predict of a child with a stage-like representation or understanding of the world."[137] Other research has shown that children can develop new problem-solving approaches, even beyond their previously observed performance levels. [138]

Research on learning suggests that children's capacities are not fixed but go ahead of what we might think they are capable of learning.[139] It also indicates that simply being exposed to different ways of thinking about a problem can be enough for children to learn new strategies. Again, these findings challenge traditional theories about children's reasoning as fixed and stage-like. The black and white concepts about stages of development limit learning are a myth, for the most part. We can learn at any age and learn in many ways. Research shows that how people think is influenced by whether they have received exposure to the types of problems they are trying to solve and given opportunities to practice thinking in new ways.[140-143] It turns out that significant learning can occur through experience and in playful contexts at any age. Children can learn at an early age, whether interacting with adults or exploring the world independently.

Early Good Habits, A Golden Opportunity!

We all have routines. Some are good, some are bad. But what does it mean to have a habit? A habit is something that we do regularly and often without thinking about it. We've done it so many times that it's become part of our daily routine. We've all heard the phrase "bad habits are hard to break." Well, that's because they are! But what if your bad habits were instead good? That's what we're talking about when it comes to routines. Routines are a vital part of the everyday lives of children and adults alike—they help us get through the day and make sure we don't forget anything important. But routines are essential for children because they allow them to grow up healthy and strong.

For example, a bedtime routine can set your child up for a good night's sleep and let everyone in your family know what to expect as you head into bedtime. Family routines support the development of social skills and academic success, and adherence to family routines is vital for family resilience during times of crisis. And there's more: observational research indicates that individuals in good health engage in highly routine health behaviors. For example, those who maintain weight loss often eat the same foods, exercise regularly, and do not skip meals. If you want to keep your body healthy and strong—and have more energy along the way—try setting some daily routines for yourself!

Publilius Syrus[144] was an enslaved Syrian who became a wealthy and respected Roman freedman in the 1st century BC. He is probably best known for his collection of witty aphorisms, called Sententiae, although we don't know anything definitive about their author or composition date. "Practice is the best of all instructors" is one Latin phrase attributed to him. Why do we still quote it after more than two thousand years? That's because it's true! It doesn't matter if you're talking about piano lessons or soccer—if you practice something enough, your skills will improve. And it goes for everything in life: if you do something repeatedly, it will eventually become a habit. It might seem like a small thing on the surface, but patterns in the form of practices are what make us who we are—at least in part. They're how we get through our days without thinking about every little thing—they just become automatic. The great thing about habits is that they are susceptible to change (or break)! If your routine isn't working for you anymore, don't be afraid to try something new! Remember: whatever new way you choose, it'll take at least 21 days to become a habit, so don't give up too soon!

With your child, you have a golden opportunity of creating good habits from the start. If not from the very beginning, it is still easier to modify a child's habit because of their capacity to learn new things. Have you ever tried to break a habit? It's not easy. It's tough. Why is that? Well, habits are actions and behaviors we perform subconsciously, so when we form and repeat habits, there are processes in the brain to make activities "first possible and then effortless." Those changes we associate with habits can become the foundation for things that we do at a higher level, as discussed when discussing freedom for excellence. One of the things happening in the brain is the release of the chemical dopamine, causing a feeling of pleasure and with it a strengthened habit. More than that, the person "as a whole" is involved in an activity that becomes familiar and easy to do—second nature. Your children must develop healthy habits from an early age.

The importance of habits is so great that it is hard to overstate their significance in a child's development. We help our children to form good habits by making healthy and good behaviors easy and fun. The foundation for good habits rests on a bed of practice. The more we can do, the easier it is. What we repeat regularly becomes ingrained in our memory systems. Good habits are like a solid foundation: they help us achieve our goals. They are rituals that lead to health and wellness across a lifetime. Create a quiet, pleasant, and refreshing home routine for your child. The habit of regular exercise is like brushing teeth: it will become effective only when you have the habit of doing it regularly. It's essential to get them into the habit of doing chores and making their bed, and it helps instill a good work ethic into them for the future. Granted, having your kid pitch in around the house can seem like an impossible task. Most children resist any kind of chore, much less regularly doing them. Believe it or not, you can train them to pick up after themselves. I'm not talking about the occasional sweep under the table or picking up their snack wrappers in the middle of the night. They will become responsible members of your household daily without much prodding.

Note that you need to set clear expectations and make it a habit to achieve consistent responsibility. There's no need to nag or fight with your kids about their responsibilities by assigning chores every day. Teach your child responsibility, good habits, and healthy living by setting an appropriate schedule for their age. Give them tasks to do as early on as possible. You should set up chores for your child to help with cleaning the house, taking care of pets, or other responsibilities so they can learn from an early age. Help them choose a morning routine, get ready for bed at night, brush their teeth and make sure they're putting their things away in the right place. These chores may seem like no big deal, but they'll give your family more peace of mind and help make it easier to get through each day (and school year!)

Help Them Believe They Are Intelligent!

Children's ideas or perceptions about their intelligence and ability affect academic performance, as well as their self-confidence and motivation. Studies indicate that mothers' positive perceptions of their children's behavior foreshadow their academic and affective functioning over time.[145] Start early and help your children believe in their intellectual potential. Tell them about their strengths and talents. Let them know that you believe in them. As adults, we can encourage our children's learning by giving them confidence in themselves and their abilities. What children already know about intelligence affects their learning. If children believe that intelligence is a fixed capacity, they will think that anyone with "little" intelligence cannot become more intelligent. If, on the other hand, children do not believe that intelligence is fixed, it opens avenues for learning about how to learn and more effective strategies for overcoming difficulties in learning. Help your children to see themselves as intelligent and capable. It is a good thing! Consistently believing that they are competent and skilled helps them build knowledge, relationships, and confidence.

What people believe about their potential affects how hard they work to achieve a goal. You'll never realize what you can do if you are too worried about being wrong or incompetent! If your children believe they can learn to write, they will be motivated to practice writing and become better writers. If your child thinks he is terrible at math, he will likely develop feelings of helplessness and dread when faced with math homework. As parents, we can help our children become confident learners by being encouraging, supportive, patient, and realistic in our expectations. Showing children, they're talented can increase their interest and motivation to learn. What we think—and what our kids believe—about intelligence makes a difference!

Context Facilitates Learning

Generalization is the foundation of learning: it's just the process of going from the specific to the general. Generalizing learning is not spontaneous but instead needs to be aided with specific teaching strategies. When teaching your child, keep in mind that context facilitates learning, and if you want them to learn something, you need to teach it in a way meaningful to them. Teaching children about the world around them gives them a better understanding of how things work. If they can see how things work in one environment, they will find it easier to apply their knowledge to other situations. Here are some suggestions for making your child's learning experiences more meaningful:

1) Give your children the opportunity to observe real-life examples of what they are studying.

2) Encourage them to ask questions to develop their understanding of the topic and help clarify what they may not understand.

3) Encourage participation in hands-on activities that allow them to apply what they learn in real-world situations.

4) Enhance your child's motivation to learn what you are teaching them (e.g., The answer to this question should be clear to the child: "Why am I learning this?").

Language In Early Childhood Education

Early language and literacy (reading and writing) development begins in the first three years of life and benefits from your child's earliest experiences with books and stories. To help a child develop language and literacy, please talk, read and sing with them. Reading and writing are essential skills for higher educational achievement and future employment. In addition, early reading helps children develop vocabulary, thinking skills, problem-solving abilities, memory skills, and self-esteem.[146-147] Pediatrics Societies encourage reading to children at home.[147,148] Language is foundational for learning. Children are born with the capacity to learn languages, but it can be more challenging for some children. Language helps children understand the world around them and make sense of their experiences. These are some additional benefits:

• Children who have good language skills will generally do better in school and are more likely to succeed later.

• Children with strong language skills are more able to follow directions and complete tasks without assistance.

• These same children will be more adept at following complex directions given by teachers or parents.

• A child who has good vocabulary skills may be better able at reading comprehension as well as writing assignments.

• Language provides a foundation for reasoning

Language, Thinking, and Learning

Language is a critical component of children's cognitive development. The more words children hear in their home environment, the more opportunities they have to learn. Language is central to thinking and learning, and language and other cognitive skills are related. Speech is a fundamental tool for learning that helps build other cognitive skills such as memory, reasoning, and problem-solving by allowing us to communicate about the things we see or experience during our day-to-day lives.

Language development is a process that starts as social interaction and gradually transforms into something else. At first, you use language to get things done and recognize objects, but eventually, it evolves into something more than this; your speech becomes a medium for self-reflection and self-awareness. By three years of age, children use language to direct their behavior using self-talk and thinking aloud, which will occur until about seven. Then around this age, a new stage begins and internalized thought appears. This internalization of thinking opens new possibilities for your child to regulate behavior. Your child reaches a new level of reflection on the reasons and motivations behind actions.

As a child, you probably remember being told to "use your words" when you were having a dispute with a sibling or classmate. But what does that mean? It turns out that using language has some pretty profound effects on the way we think and act. As children develop language, they gain new capacities to reflect and plan by facilitating their mental consideration of alternatives before acting. Language and memory work together to assist the young child's developing abilities to think and plan based on past experiences. At the same time, they also consider the future consequences of their actions, and language helps them remember what happened before to make better decisions. At this age, new opportunities for teaching are open for parents and teachers alike.

Language and Executive Functions

What is the correlation between language and executive functions? Well, according to some studies, it's pretty high. Studies that assess the correlation between language and executive functions in preschoolers have generally found positive correlations between measures of executive function and verbal ability at this early age. The most important executive functions[149] include:

1. Inhibition—being able to restrain one's impulsive or instinctive reactions.

2. Attentional flexibility in applying ideas or rules.

3. Working memory, the ability to hold information in mind while processing it.

Each of these executive functions is vital to how children develop self-regulatory abilities, which enable them to become effective learners. Below we will look at several topics and tips about training executive functions, including a vital skill, the capacity for "thinking about your thinking."

Talking and Listening

As our language develops, we learn to listen to other people and understand. When your child is a baby, the way they can communicate with the world around them is mostly through crying. They'll learn how to talk and use gestures and facial expressions to express themselves as they get older. Speaking and listening are like music—silence can be as expressive as the sounds when used skillfully. Learning how to listen is just as important as learning how to speak—and it's a skill that takes time to develop. Children become better listeners as they get older.

INSTRUCTION

Listening skills require practice, games, or activities that encourage children to pay attention while someone else speaks strengthens those skills. You can model listening for your child by paying close attention, nodding your head, and making eye contact. When you play games like "Simon Says" or "Red Light Green Light," you'll find that your child will have fun while learning how to listen closely!

You can also help your child build their listening skills by reading aloud daily and asking them questions about what they heard. By doing so, you will be helping them develop their language skills and their ability to comprehend what they have just heard. Children need to know how conversations work to understand what others are saying, including knowing when it is their turn to speak and when someone else is talking. You can help your child learn these rules by modeling good behavior during conversations with family members or friends on the phone.

Encourage your child to listen by asking questions like: "What did you hear?" or "What do you think?" If they answer incorrectly, ask them why they thought something different from what was said. This type of interaction helps children realize that their interpretation of what someone is saying may not always be correct—that there are other possibilities besides theirs! You may also encourage your child to listen by setting aside time each day, free from distractions, so they can focus on listening. Start with short periods (10 minutes) until they get used to it; then increase the duration as they become more comfortable.

Speaking and Reading

As parents, it's essential to focus on the importance of speaking and reading to your children. You can do this by talking to them about what they see or reading from a book or magazine with difficult words for them to understand. They'll be able to learn new things when you explain the meaning of difficult words straightforwardly. As children grow older and develop their language skills, they will understand how people communicate with each other through various modes of communication such as speech and writing. These new skills help them develop better social skills and improve their language usage. They can now express themselves more accurately than before without difficulty at all!

There's no such thing as too much talking when raising children. You know what I'm talking about: when you're out with your kids and they start asking questions like, "What's that?" or "Why is that person so funny looking?" and tell them the answer, but they still don't seem satisfied. You realize that your little ones don't just want to hear you speak—they want to listen! And once you've got them listening, it's time to teach them how to understand what other people are saying by asking questions about what they heard and read. For example, if someone says something in a foreign language or uses a word that's difficult for children to understand, ask them what they think it means before giving a definition or explanation (that way, it will stick). You can also help them learn new words by reading books or magazines with difficult vocabulary words so they can practice on their own time. Once your child understands how people communicate through speech and writing, their social skills will improve, and they'll be able to express themselves more accurately than before without having any difficulty at all!

Writing Skills

Let's face it: writing is hard. It's a skill that develops over time and takes lots of practice. And while there are lots of ways to practice writing, you probably don't want to be doing it all day long. But if you're like most people, you need it in your life. Writing is a skill that develops over time. Children are just learning how to form letters and sounds in the early years, which means they need lots of practice making shapes with their hands. Later in school, when you're getting ready to write essays in your English class, you may wish there had been more hours in the day to have spent more time studying and practicing writing skills. Writing is critical because it helps us express ourselves clearly and because it's a skill required for schoolwork (e-mailing professors), work (writing reports), and many other functions.

When we write something down, we must think about what we want to say before putting it on paper or typing it into a computer. This process helps us organize our thoughts to make sense to others who read them later! Writing skills are a powerful tool that will benefit your child in many ways in the future. From early on, children can learn to communicate by writing. From drawing pictures to scribbling letters, they will use their writing skills throughout their lives. Research suggests that when we teach children to read and write early on, they do better in school.[150]

Music

Gregorian chants, Bach, Mozart, Beethoven. Throughout its history, Western art music has evolved from simple songs and chants to the complex musical forms of today. Around the ninth century, monks began singing them at Masses and other important events in their monasteries to praise God. Gregorian chants have influenced many composers throughout history because they write music using only simple melodies and harmonies. Bach, Mozart, and Beethoven are culminating examples of the magnificent musical heritage of Western Civilization. Today we have access to music from the past and the present from around the world.

The development of music in the child parallels its development in history! From mama's lullabies to more complex forms, every child needs to have access to music. For most of us, music brings great joy to our lives. It helps us relax, soothes pain and discomfort, and can bring back pleasant memories and emotions. Music is vital to every child's development; it teaches children how to listen. The first sounds we hear as newborns are mama's lullabies or other soothing sounds that soothe us and help us feel safe in the world. As a parent, you want to give your children the best possible chance in life. One way you can do that is by exposing them early on to inspiring music, beautiful music that has passed the test of time. Music has been proven to help develop cognitive function, motor control, and memory skills, and even improved language skills! If anything, music has the potential to unify love, discipline, creativity and freedom, instruction, and worldview aspects uniquely. Do you see any musical talent in your children? Cultivate it!

What is "Inductive Reasoning"?

Inductive reasoning is proceeding from particular facts to a general conclusion. When you fall, it's like the world is falling apart. When someone else falls, you think that it hurts them. Even though you are not absolutely sure that is the case, induction allows you to draw a general conclusion with some confidence—which is good enough for most everyday situations. One of the main learning pathways for infants and young children is this way of learning. Sorting toys by shape, color, or size is an example of using inductive reasoning to learn about the world around them. Children learn first through their senses, ears, eyes, and body sensations. Inductive reasoning helps a child put together individual pieces of information to form a larger picture or make a connection between different ideas. We can see this kind of reasoning when toddlers make predictions by observing cause and effect with objects. When children are encouraged to predict or conclude something based on prior knowledge and experience, they engage in inductive reasoning.

Thus, inductive reasoning is the process of using previous knowledge to make sense of new information. It is an essential part of how children learn. For example, if your child sees you play the violin and asks you to play it again, you may think that your child is learning by imitating behavior. However, they use inductive reasoning to make a commonsense generalization about how things work. How many times have you heard a small child ask why something is the way it is? Chances are that you could hardly remember the last time you didn't hear one. This is because when children learn about their world, they want to understand their place in it and how everything relates to them. When they look at animals, they wonder what they are like. When they look at plants and flowers, they wonder where they come from.

Children can learn about the world around them by exploring, observing, and interacting with objects in their environment (e.g., pushing buttons on a toy or hitting keys on a piano). Through inductive reasoning, children's minds develop in ways that are meaningful to them at that time. This type of reasoning helps children understand cause and effect relationships and how objects relate to one another when they are taken together within their environment or even inside different containers. Thus, inductive reasoning is a form of learning in which, from specific examples, a general rule becomes clear. We see this when children learn to draw letters and then, later, whole words. Inductive learning begins with observing one or two things and can include many observations. Stimulate this form of reasoning and learning in your child. It will become a way to develop creative ideas and new solutions!

Metacognition

Did you know that metacognition[151] is one of the most important skills you can teach your child? It's true! Metacognition is a hot topic in the world of teaching and learning. You've probably heard the term 'metacognition' before, but maybe you don't know what it means. Or perhaps you do, but you still don't see how important it is to teach your child. Metacognition is "the self-regulation of cognition, which allows individuals to adaptively regulate their cognitive processes in order to maximize performance and learning in real-world settings."[137] Metacognition is also the capacity to monitor, assess, control, and change how one thinks and learns.

Metacognition is just a fancy word for "thinking about your thinking." Teaching your child how to learn includes a group of practices that enhance your child's learning capacities. When your children have metacognitive skills, they can better understand what they don't know and use their knowledge to seek out new information. They are also better able to set goals for themselves and determine when they have learned enough from a task (or when they have mastered it). Development in this area enables them to be more independent learners and gives them confidence when tackling new challenges!

Children need to think about their thinking and learn how to learn because this will help them solve problems in the future. If metacognition is the ability to think about your thinking, it then means that it's also the skill that allows you to think about how you're thinking. This ability means that metacognition is a skill you use while you're using other skills—it's like a meta-skill. It's also what makes you wonder whether you should be thinking about this right now. (You should.) There are strategies to help children develop metacognitive skills. If you want to teach your child such skills, you can use some of them!

—Active listening[152] strategies: What does this have to do with listening? Well, when we listen, we're using many different skills: comprehension, critical thinking, problem-solving, and communication, to name a few. But did you know there are specific ways we can listen more effectively? That's right: active listening strategies! You can use active listening with your children to have them listen attentively. Simple yet effective strategies include turning your body directly toward the child; making eye contact; questioning; nodding when appropriate; repeating what the child said to you; and more! Parents can teach and model active listening strategies for their children, so they develop these metacognitive skills and internalize them for future use.

—Teach your child how to think about what they are learning. For example, if they are reading a book, ask them questions like: "What do you think will happen after this?" or "Why did she do that?"

—Help your child reflect on their own learning experiences. Ask them questions like: "What did you enjoy most about that lesson? What new skills did you learn? What was difficult for you? How can you do it better next time?

—Self-questioning is one way to train metacognition in your child: Self-questioning involves pausing during a task to check your actions consciously. Help your child ask important questions like: Is there something important that I miss? Did I do it the best way? And even, how can I think better about what I'm doing?

—Mnemonic aids[153] are strategies you can use to improve information retention. Rhymes, patterns, and associations to remember are traditional ways to help remember. These are ways of adding context (additional or surrounding information) to a fact to help you recall it. Other methods include Rhyme, Association, Pattern, Alphabetical order (first letter), or Visual association (color).

For instance, this is a fun way to teach kids to count to twenty: One, Two, buckle my shoe, Three, Four, knock at the door, Five, Six, pick up sticks, Seven, Eight, Lay them straight, Nine, Ten, a big fat hen, Eleven, Twelve, dig and delve, Thirteen, Fourteen, maids a-courting, Fifteen, Sixteen, maids in the kitchen, Nineteen, Twenty, my plate's empty. Or the great lakes: Superior, Michigan, Huron, Erie, and Ontario with the phrase: Super Man Helps Everyone. Let's say you meet a singer named John. You teach your child this sentence "John will sing a song before long." With this aid, recalling both his name and profession will be easy!

—Journals:[154] Another way to enhance metacognition is through journals. Create one with your children as an assignment at the end of each day or week where you can help them write down what went well and what didn't go well at school that day/weekend for them.

—Graphic organizers: These tools help us organize our thoughts, create connections between things we know, think more deeply about something, visualize processes and procedures, etc. Here are some examples:

1) Mind maps: A mind map is a graphic organizer that allows you to spill your thoughts onto a sheet or screen and shuffle and sort your ideas to help you organize your mind better. By using a graphic organizer like this, you're more effectively thinking about your thinking!

2) Flow charts: A flow chart is a diagram consisting of boxes or circles connected by lines that show how something works step-by-step (or as one big circle). You can use them for anything—to plan a vacation or project, figure out how to get somewhere new without getting lost on public transportation (like subways), etc.

—Active reading strategies —reading is essential— ensure that while they read, they are concentrating and comprehending the information they are reading. Active reading is about focus and determination for understanding and evaluating the written work for its relevance to your needs. Examples include underlining important information or scanning for main ideas.

—Reciprocal teaching:[154] This approach emphasizes four more strategies you can teach your child to practice:

(1) question generating: questioning yourself or asking friends questions to check comprehension.

(2) summarizing: summarizing texts in one or two sentences after reading.

(3) predicting: predicting how a story will go by looking at pictures on the cover.

(4) clarifying: clarifying when something doesn't make sense by asking for clarification from friends or a teacher rather.

Teaching your child to be a self-sufficient learner is one of the most important things you can do for them. It's also an essential skill for children because it's not just about school—it's about life!

Learning and Motivation

You might think learning and motivation are closely related. And you're right! They work together to get the job done. Learning and motivation work together, but it's important to remember that they're not the same thing. Motivation gets you to do something—it's what makes you want to learn. It can be intrinsic (I'm interested in this) or extrinsic (I need to know this). But learning isn't just about motivation—it's also about understanding what you're learning and using that knowledge. And motivation is what helps you get into the right headspace for both of those things!

We all know that motivation is key to learning, but did you know that self-regulation is a big part of what motivates us? Carol Susan Dweck is an American professor of Psychology at Stanford University. In a study by Dweck,[155] researchers gave children a puzzle to play with. They told some of the children they were smart while telling the others they were not so smart. The 'smart' kids kept trying to solve the puzzle until they got it right, whereas the 'not-so-smart' kids gave up after a few tries. The 'smart' kids also thought they could improve their ability by practicing more, while the 'not-so-smart' kids thought they could never get any better at solving puzzles. This disposition is called self-efficacy and affects how much effort we put into something—whether it's learning or anything else in life!

Motivation is all about how you feel about learning. It's why you choose to do it, and it's what makes you want to keep on doing it. It can be external — for example, when someone else rewards you for learning, or internal — like when you just like doing something because it feels good. When motivation is strong, you feel like education is fun and easy; it can seem like a chore when it's weak. Self-regulation is how well we control ourselves. It's how much we stick with our goals even when things get tough and how well we plan so that we know what needs doing next (i.e., "sequencing"). Self-regulation also means dealing with distractions without losing track of where we were before they happened, such as putting your phone away while working on homework!

Here are some tips that might help you learn to motivate your child (yourself or others!) in genuinely effective ways:

1. Ask yourself what your goals are. Clarifying this may seem simple, but it's essential to know what you're working towards before working towards it. If you don't know where you're going, how will you know when you've arrived?

· INSTRUCTION ·

2. Consider how much effort each goal may take to complete and how much time is available for those efforts to occur. If there's not enough time or energy for both tasks, prioritize accordingly! You don't want to be wasting precious resources on things that aren't important enough for their own sake anyway.

3. Make sure whatever steps are needed are clear enough to be completed without confusion or misunderstanding! In the absence of clear instructions and goals, things can go wrong. It's crucial to ensure everyone knows what needs to happen at each step.

4. Motivation tends to develop and then surge as you start working on something. Psychologist Rubin Khoddam explains: "The motivation trap, as stated by Dr. Russ Harris states that we wait to feel motivated before we take any action. Now you might be asking, what's the problem with that? The problem is that if you're always waiting for motivation to hit, you may be waiting your whole. While you're waiting on motivation, motivation is waiting on you. Because committed action comes first and motivation comes second."[156]

Don't think that you must be highly motivated before you can start that project you've wanted to do for a long time.

Reading this book tells of your motivation for your child's upbringing. But as an adult, maybe you struggle with a lack of motivation for something significant you would like to accomplish. One symptom of lack of motivation can be procrastination. You may have the talent and the training to achieve more than you have. Maybe you are a perfectionist, and it would be emotionally more acceptable to avoid a project or reaching for a goal than to face the uncertainty and the possibility of not doing whatever it is well. You may be concerned about how others will judge you in case of failure. This self-sabotage operates through an underlying sense of sub-conscious insecurity. If this is the case, try to understand the root of the problem and what is causing the insecurity. Another cause of procrastination (and lack of motivation) is related to difficulty breaking bad habits. Now going back to motivation and your child, note the importance of establishing good habits and instilling self-confidence to prevent procrastination and help your child operate with healthy levels of motivation.

Memory

When you observe your child growing, developing, and learning, always remember it is something extraordinary. They are just echoing to you the words of the Psalmist: "...I am fearfully and wonderfully made..."[157] The brain is a magnificent organ, and it is capable of incredible feats, from controlling your entire body to remembering where you left your keys. Each person's brain has about 86 billion neurons and over ten trillion synapses. It performs a whopping ten quadrillion calculations (1 with 16 zeros) per second. Some 10 to 50 other units called glial cells provide structural support, resources, and immune protection for each neuron. You may say teamwork! In total, counting neurons and all other cells, there is a staggering number of cells in the brain: 180 billion![158]

Have you ever wondered what happens in your child's brain when they learn something? Let's look at those fundamental building units of our brains—the cell called a neuron. Synapses are tiny gaps between neurons that transmit chemical messages from one cell to another. When an electrical signal travels down one neuron's prolongation (axons) and reaches the synapse, the released chemicals (called neurotransmitters) go into the space between the two cells. These neurotransmitters then bind with receptors on the other neuron and send another electrical signal into its dendrite.

Hebbian learning[159] is part of the memory-forming process in the brain. In essence, neurons that fire together near simultaneously in time wire together. In other words, neurons and networks of neurons that respond together to certain events tend to link together. Using an analogy, they will sing to the same tune, in unison, like a choir. Donald Hebb, a Canadian psychologist, first described this process. Hebbian learning happens as the brain forms new connections every time we learn something new or recall an old memory. Whenever you or your child learn a new fact, concept, or procedure, new relationships between sets of neurons form in the brain.

When we first learn something new (like how to ride a bike), these connections are fragile and not very strong yet (like when you first started riding). At first, there were many bumps and scrapes, but eventually, you could ride without even thinking about it! There happens a transition from short-term to long-term memory. These connections develop when neurons fire messages to one another. So, every time you repeat something over again—whether it's learning how to ride a bike or memorizing multiplication tables—connections between certain groups of neurons are strengthened. When children learn something new, they often do it repeatedly until it becomes automatic, this is memory consolidation. Consolidation allows memories to become long-term memory to be easily accessed later without having to re-learn them from scratch. The more these connections are activated, the stronger they become—and the easier it is for your child to recall them later.

Short-term memory allows us to hold seven plus items in our mind at once for only 20 seconds before we forget them. Long-term memory[160] allows us to store information for long periods. The brain can increase or decrease the number of connections and sometimes the number of cells (for instance, in the hippocampus, concerning memory and learning). This creation of new synapses or even new cells is called synaptic plasticity. This plasticity is essential for learning; without it, we would not be able to learn anything new!

Short-term memory is your brain's way of storing data while processing it. It's like a scratchpad that your mind can use to work out problems and make decisions. For example, if you're trying to figure out how many gallons of paint you need to cover your bedroom walls, you'll probably start by thinking about the size of the room and how much paint you may need for each partition. When you've got all the numbers in your head, you can move on to long-term memory,[160] and your memory bank and metacognitive skills will assist in deciding or calculating. Here is where working memory—a different form of memory—enters to help. Working memory is like a go-between your short-term and long-term memory, and it is essential for executive functioning and for following instructions and paying attention. Here is where things get interesting! Long-term memory isn't just one thing—it consists of different components that work together to form a cohesive whole. We see one more example of metacognition in action in all of this!

Another subdivision of memory includes explicit (or declarative) and implicit (or procedural). Implicit memories underlie habits and other skills we call upon without even thinking about them, for example, when you ride a bike or drive a car on autopilot. Explicit memories are facts, events, and experiences that we consciously recall, for example, where you went on vacation last year or what grade point average you got in high school math class. Memory allows us to travel across time, remember things from the past, and even remember things we envisioned for our future. Short-term memory is essential for using information that we need to recall in the short term, like a new phone number or the answer to a question. On the other hand, long-term memory allows us to retain information over time, like the lyrics to your favorite song or the multiplication tables you learned in elementary school.

Short-Term to Long-Term

Now, this is something I would like to emphasize. Short-term and long-term memory are both necessary for learning, and the transition between short and long-term memory is an essential aspect of learning. However, to have memories consolidated in long-term memory can be tricky—at least in one regard. Often students fool themselves into thinking they learn something without actually committing it to long-term memory, only to find out later that it has vanished from their minds. They then go back over what happened and discover that they never committed the information to long-term memory in the first place. Research has shown that most students think they have learned something without saving it to long-term memory, only to be later disappointed!

How do I help my child learn with long-term memory in mind? To convert short-term memory into long-term, train your child to do the following:

(1) Pay attention to new information and make a conscious effort to remember it.

(2) Organize the information to aid in memory retention.

(3) Associate it with already-known information putting it in a larger context.

(4) Repeat the information over time to internalize it and make it familiar.

(5) Prompt your child to retrieve recently learned things.

(6) Teach your child healthy lifestyle habits and physical exercise to keep the brain in good shape.

(7) Encourage mentally stimulating activities like reading and learning about exciting things!

One Last Word

Parents need to challenge their children by having high expectations for them without being unrealistic. Parents should give their children work that requires focused and sustained effort—that way, they'll feel challenged and inspired to figure out how to do it. When children study material that is too easy, they'll fall into a routine where they don't learn anything new or improve their existing knowledge base. For instance, most video games have fuzzy objectives to better model real-life scenarios and challenges. Ask questions to know what your children have learned and stimulate their curiosity. Like the best teachers, use explanation to keep your children on their toes—challenging them to think about problems in new ways. A good teacher will find a way to turn something complicated into something simple by using examples, analogies, or other methods. The goal is to get your children to understand complex concepts in a way that makes sense to them. When teaching your children, show them how to do things and do them better and more efficiently. Modeling is what experts call it—the generous sharing of your expertise so that your children can benefit from it and develop their skills. And finally, practice makes perfect; it helps consolidate memories and improve skills. It leaves you and your child with a sense of accomplishment.

For excellence and a competitive edge, consider that parents of exceptionally resilient and successful kids always do the following:[161]

- Have patience when their children ask questions.
- Push their children to play to their strengths.
- Demonstrate the link between hard work and extraordinary outcomes.

They create a culture of striving and excellence.

WORLDVIEW

"Miracles are a retelling in small letters of the very same story which is written across the whole world in letters too large for some of us to see."[162]
—C.S. Lewis

What is a worldview? It's a question that has been asked—in different ways—by just about every human being at one point or another. The World seems like a pretty big place, and we want to know what it means—why we're here, how we should live, what our ultimate destiny could be, and so on. But what is a worldview? In short: it's your answer to those big questions. Your worldview is an overall way of looking at the World, its origin and purpose, and understanding how it works. Your worldview might depend on religion or philosophy, or both—but no matter where it comes from, your worldview is what guides you through life. It is not just about beliefs but also practices and behaviors. Worldviews can be religious or secular; they can be individual or communal; they can incorporate science and faith; they can be old or new; they can be black or white; they can be true or false.

When we look at the world, we see a multitude of things. But our worldview guides how we perceive and interpret reality. Our worldview determines what we think is important, what we believe is truthful, and what actions we take. It is vital to have a coherent and truth-based worldview—because it unifies many aspects that otherwise would be dispersed and incoherent. Such a worldview helps us participate in the accumulated wisdom of generations past and gives us a framework for understanding our place in the world. It helps us answer the most critical questions in life: "Who am I?" "What does it mean to live? What should be my purpose on Earth?" "What is truth?" "How should I live my life?" And it may also inform you about morality and ethical decisions: "What does it mean to be good?" "What does it mean to be evil?" "How do we define these things?" "What is my moral duty when faced with an emergency?" "How do I balance my safety with helping others?" "What will bring me fulfillment during my life on this earth?" and so on.

The word "worldview" comes from the German Weltanschauung (literally "world view"), which German philosopher Immanuel Kant first used in his Critique of Pure Reason (1781).[163] He defined the term as "the sum total of all our judgments upon experience"[163]. Therefore, a worldview is a system or set of ideas that we use to explain reality and make sense of it. It helps us understand reality in general terms, its composition, how things change over time, and why they happen. You know what I'm talking about. For instance, you're watching a movie, and you can't stand how the main character is acting. Or you're reading a book, and you think the author made the main character do something foolish. That's your worldview at work.

A worldview[164] is a collection of attitudes, values, stories, and expectations about the World around us. It informs our every thought and action. When you encounter a situation and think, 'That's just wrong, your worldview is active. Worldview is engaged in ethics (how we act), religion (what we believe), philosophy (how we seek to understand reality), scientific beliefs (what we accept as scientific truth regarding the natural world), etc. A worldview is a belief system that helps us make sense of the World and organize our thoughts into a coherent whole. It is an expanded and distilled product of a multitude of processes of metacognition as they operate throughout our lives.

A worldview is an overall perspective on reality—how we make sense of everything around us. It's how we understand our place in the World, what we believe about God and things in the Universe, how we think about the natural and the supernatural, science and history, basically everything! All worldviews share certain core beliefs regardless of whether they belong to certain traditions or not (such as belief in an objective truth). As children grow up and reflect on the nature of knowledge and how we know what we claim to know, one of their most central questions will be, "What is Truth?" Other significant questions are: "What is the purpose of human life?" "Who can I trust?" "What is real?" "How do I know right from wrong?" "What happens after we die?" etc.

A worldview answers questions about how we fit into the larger scheme of things—and when you look at it that way, it becomes clear how much influence such beliefs have over every aspect of our lives. Your worldview is like a set of glasses—it filters everything you see through it and determines what's important to you. It helps you interpret the World around you and sort out what is of the highest value from what is least.

Tying It All Together

The main principles delineated in this book: Love, Discipline, Freedom, and Instruction will work together and strengthen each other when they are part of a coherent whole, in our case, a Worldview that has produced fruits for more than two thousand years. Its principles and values are familiar to us to different degrees—consciously or without realizing it—because they derive from our historical and cultural inheritance. Many of them flow from the highest ideals of Western Civilization.

This book aims to highlight principles applicable to the education of your child but also to your adult life. I hope they become more accessible to parents (or future parents) like you so that they may shape the education of our children and continue to guide us into the future. This book is about how our children, and we can benefit from a coherent worldview that unifies the application of these four principles—love, discipline, freedom, and instruction and how we can concretely apply them in our daily lives to make them more accurate and plentiful. We may rediscover ideas that have been developed over centuries until becoming part of our culture and thought patterns. I hope this condensed perspective will help you reclaim these principles from Greek philosophy and Judeo-Christian tradition and apply them conscientiously in your children's education.

Crisis in Our Culture

We live in an age of confusion about what is good or bad behavior, what is right or wrong, what should be true or false, how we should live our lives; how we should treat others; what it means to be human. In the late 1960s and 1970s, Canadians and Americans worried that their nation's youth were growing up too fast. They believed that young people lacked good values, engaged in sex and drugs, cared little about politics or religion, and had become emotionally distant from their parents.

In the book "Lost in Transition," subtitled: The Dark Side of Emerging Adulthood,[165] Notre Dame sociologist Christian Smith and his collaborators argue that these worries were well founded—and more than 40 years later, they remain so. They reviewed the literature about American youth over the past four decades, revealing the persistence of a wide range of moral problems among young people—including rising rates of divorce and cohabitation, declining engagement with religion and civic life, higher levels of narcissism and materialism than older generations have seen before them.

In "Lost in Transition" the authors explored moral reasoning among 18- to 23-year-old students and identified "five major problems facing very many young people today: confused moral reasoning, routine intoxication, materialistic life goals, regrettable sexual experiences, and disengagement from civic and political life….The trouble does not lie only with the emerging adults… but has much deeper roots in…a culture that emerging adults have largely inherited rather than created."[165] Since then, the situation has only gotten worse.

What should parents do? In postmodern culture, we have gone from being a people of faith and vision to mere consumers or worse. What are the implications of this? What should parents do? This book guides parents in what is essential for educating their children to live their lives with confidence, meaning, and purpose. We should not forget that Western Civilization's worldview is time-tested. Granted, it is not perfect—none is—but Western Civilization has given us a worldview that unifies in a coherent whole the four principles we have considered throughout the previous chapters.

Western civilization has given us many things: the value of human redemption, the value of the human person, and democracy, for example. It gave us science and medicine, philosophy and art, and some of the greatest thinkers and writers: Plato, Aristotle, Saint Paul of Tarsus, Saint Augustine, Saint Thomas Aquinas, Dante Alighieri, Cervantes, and Shakespeare, Leon Tolstoy, and Fyodor Dostoevsky. Let us now consider the principles of love, discipline, freedom, and instruction from the larger perspective of a particular worldview.

Love in Western Civilization

Western civilization is notable in its love for the idea of love. From Plato's Symposium to the Song of Songs of Solomon, from Ovid's Metamorphoses to the Letters of Saint Paul, from Dante's Paradiso, from Spenser's Faerie Queene to Milton's Paradise Lost, love has been so central to our culture and development that it is impossible to separate the two. Of course, this is not just true in literature: look at any great painting or sculpture, listen to any great piece of music, watch any great movie or play—you'll find love at the core of it all. At the center, the embodiment of the God that is love in the person of Christ is paramount. And it's no coincidence: Western civilization developed through the transformation of the Greco-Latin world by Judaism and Christianity, both of which rest on the understanding that God is Love itself. The Bible says that "God is love"[166] and—in one of its most familiar passages—it declares: "For God so loved the world, that He gave His only Son, so that everyone who believes in Him will not perish, but have eternal life."[167]

As discussed in Chapter 1, Western civilization gave rise to a deeper, differentiated understanding of love. There are different kinds of love:

- Eros (which focuses on sexual desire).
- Agape (which focuses on willing the good of the other).
- Philia (friendship).
- Storge (parental love).

They are not all equal—but they all have value differently. These forms of love have found a diversity of expressions throughout the history of the Western World. It's no accident that Western Civilization has been the source of outstanding achievements in human history. Love is not just a powerful driving force but also a salt—that preserves and flavors—and light that exposes, illuminates, and guides. We are talking about a profound understanding of the World that commands us to love our family, friends, and enemies. The same love compels us not to surrender to evil. Love makes us learn about new things and share what we know with others. For some, Western civilization is about war and conquest; for others, its most defining components are love, forgiveness, mercy, compassion, creativity, and institutions like the family, government, and nation—all the things that make us human. If you take away the beauty in our architecture, literature, and music and the values they instill in us—love, forgiveness, mercy, service, the impulse to create—we would have nothing essential left to treasure and conserve.

In Western civilization, love has been a powerful force for good. It has inspired us to create works of art, music, architecture, and literature that are beautiful and enduring. Many believe that love is a feeling or a sentiment, but it is more than that. But what is "love"? Admittedly, love is hard to define, and love is more than a sentiment, feeling, or affection. In the words of Saint Thomas Aquinas, one helpful concept of love is this: "Love is to will the good of the other."[168] This central understanding of love will help you educate your child and grow your relationships.

Love is not primary depending on feelings, which are not directly under your control. It is closer to an act of the will, something not elusive and even as variable as your feelings. This clear understanding can help you grow in the practice of love. It will guide you in helping your child grow and mature in developing this virtue. Love always involves some form of volition—that is, a choice to act for or against someone. Our choices are powerful because they are not just about us; they also affect others. We can choose to help someone, or we can choose not to help them. But whatever our choice, it has consequences that ripple out into the world around us and in time.

This concept of love is at the heart of all things good in Western civilization: democracy and human rights come from it; hospitals and universities come from it; science and art spring from it; even theology relies on it! Without this sense of love as an active choice for another person and their well-being, we would have no basis for understanding anything about ourselves or our World. The idea that the ultimate reality is love is powerful and transformative. If we pay attention, we will hear a call to be an ambassador of that reality to our children and the World!

Charity is one of the most important ideas to come out of the West. It is a historical fact that the Christian spirit of mutual love and communal charity was one of the most remarkable things about Western civilization. Christians cared for their poor, widows and orphans, and their sick and dying—even while dying themselves from the plague. It's easy to take hospitals for granted. After all, they're everywhere—and they seem to be an unshakable fixture of our culture. But it wasn't always this way. Christians set up the early hospitals to care for those abandoned by the state or left to die with no one to care for them.

The idea of a hospital as we know it today was born in Western civilization. For instance, by 580 AD, Christians in Spain founded a hospital at Merida—a town in the Province of Badajoz—where they would care for the sick, whether they were Christian or Jew, enslaved person or free.[169-171] This idea spread quickly throughout Europe, and by 1000 AD, there were over three hundred hospitals across the continent. Today we have thousands of hospitals in the United States and Canada alone! Christianity taught people about compassion for others, which was an entirely new idea for many people. It also brought about a new way of looking at death: instead of hiding from it or trying to avoid it at all costs, people began accepting death as part of life itself for a meaningful purpose.

Finally, Christianity taught people how to love each other—however strange that may sound in our culture today!

Discipline and Moderation

The idea of virtue has a rich tradition in the West. From Plato's ancient Greeks to Aristotle to Christianity, Westerners have always been interested in what it means to be a good person. Plato lived in the fourth century B.C., and he identified four virtues that have become influential concepts in Western civilization. Now known as the four cardinal virtues, they are wisdom, courage, moderation, and justice. Aristotle, Plato's student, expanded the concept by including additional virtues. With Christianity, the idea reached new heights as part of a novel Worldview. This vision linked the hope of life after death with helping others in the "here and now." Christians who believed most strongly in the life to come did the most to improve the situation of people living in this life.

For the first time in history, the Christian Worldview integrated love, discipline, moderation, and freedom into a comprehensive answer to the main existential questions. Its explanatory power resonated with the realities of human life, the most profound needs, and people's highest aspirations. One of the pillars of Western civilization is the cultivation of discipline and moderation—a general attitude of a due mean between extremes—a set of moral standards, habits, and practices that guide how we should live our lives.

Discipline and moderation are a misunderstood pair of words. We often hear things like discipline and moderation are synonyms with punishment, suppression, or repression; they are expressions of cowardice and a lack of passion, or discipline and moderation are boring. It is time to clear up some of the confusion. First, discipline and moderation are not ends in themselves. They're means to higher ends: happiness, achievement, and spiritual growth. Second, discipline and moderation don't mean punishment, suppression, or repression. There is no question that we could use them for that purpose—but if you've ever met someone who has a lot of self-control, you know that it doesn't make them any less passionate about what they're doing. When people have self-control, they can be passionate about things because they don't waste their energy on things that aren't important to them. Thirdly, discipline and moderation are not cowardly. Quite the opposite: by focusing on what's most important to us (and keeping ourselves from getting distracted by other things), we can be bolder than someone who doesn't have those same qualities! Discipline and moderation are a way of living that embraces the best in you: your intelligence, creativity, and passion for life. It's not about suppressing or repressing those things—it's about channeling them in healthy ways that allow you to live an entire, happy life of achievements.

Whether you have a career, a happy marriage, or kids to educate, discipline is about more than following rules or being neat and orderly. It's also about having the self-control to do what you need to do when you need to do it—even if you don't feel like it or want to do it. Discipline means sticking with your plans even when they get hard. Discipline means doing what you've planned even when other people might think differently and doing the right thing even when no one else is watching or paying attention—which means that discipline can take many forms:

- Keeping a budget.
- Getting up early every day.
- Going to work on time every day.
- Sometimes is keeping a promise that you made even when there is no material reward in doing it.

- The self-control that begins early in life as self-discipline and can translate into control of undesirable thoughts later in life, a foundation for maturity.

So, if you've been thinking about trying out more discipline and moderation for yourself but were worried it might be boring or mundane, don't worry! You will be defeating procrastination and pursuing your goals. Paradoxically, you can become more ambitious, passionate, and creative through discipline and moderation!

Freedom

Western civilization is both timeless and constantly changing. The past lives on in the present in a multitude of forms, and the future is always just around the corner with new synthesis. The Western tradition is not just about fighting for freedom or democracy; it's about creating something beautiful where there was once nothing but chaos. It's about combining all these ideas—from religion to art, science to law—into one cohesive whole. Despite its many flaws, the real triumph of this civilization lies in taking diverse and seemingly inconsistent bodies of knowledge and weaving them into a pattern of ideas that harmonizes and gives strength to its components. When it comes to freedom, lighthouses shine in different times and places. José Martí said: "Man loves liberty, even if he does not know that he loves it. He is driven by it and flees from where it does not exist"[172] and "Liberty is the right of every man, to be honest, to think and to speak without hypocrisy."[172] The West has produced a unique synthesis that speaks to the human mind and soul in a way that elevates not only the individual but an entire civilization.

Let us briefly look at the roots of freedom in Western civilization. Greek philosophers believed that humans were rational beings with an innate search for truth and knowledge; they also believed that humans should learn to use their reason correctly. But the roots of freedom in Western civilization can be traced back even farther than this—back to ancient Israel when Moses led his people out of slavery in Egypt through the desert to Mount Sinai, where he received God's Ten Commandments from God. Himself! These commandments included commands against murder, adultery, coveting, theft, etc. You might have not thought of them as a prescription for freedom but in essence, that is what they are. Imagine how free society would be if the Ten Commandments were written in the hearts of people!

Christianity can be said to have given us our freedom by its emphasis at the same time on community and on individual salvation and its impact on philosophy, which led to later social respect for the dignity of the human person. A long history of subsequent philosophic developments added new contributions to understanding the different dimensions of freedom. Similarly, Hebrew emphasis on the original goodness of this World and its fallen condition implies that humans have God-given freedom to choose between good and evil. This freedom is considered a precondition for a loving relationship with God the Creator. At the heart of Christianity is love, and a relationship based on love demands freedom as a necessary condition. The Hebrews and Christians recognized that humans are a creation in the image of God—one central concept—and that this meant they could make decisions by themselves—not necessarily because they wanted to do so, but because they were capable of doing so. All these ideas contributed to future humanitarian, social, and political improvements.

The Hebrew influence (as contrasted with the Greek) expressed later through Christianity strengthened freedom. By emphasizing such factors as the importance of time and change, history, and the individual's responsibility before God and in relationship with others. Most influential Greek thinkers belittled these aspects. These concepts were later developed further by thinkers like the British John Locke (1632-1704),[173] who argued that all people are born equal with natural rights, including life, liberty, and property. These ideas became central to Western society as they grew over time.

New aspirations developed in the hearts and minds of thinkers and people. Freedom from oppression and tyranny; freedom from want and need; freedom from fear and terror; freedom from wanton destruction; freedom for all people regardless of gender, race, class, or creed. The United States Declaration of Independence succinctly and beautifully reflects the attractiveness of these values: "We hold these truths to be self-evident, that all men are created equal, that their Creator endows them with certain unalienable Rights, that among these are Life, Liberty and the pursuit of Happiness."[174]

Freedom of Thought and Speech

It's easy to assume that the idea of Freedom of Conscience is a modern invention; however, the roots of this idea stretch back over 2,000 years. The concept is developed throughout the Bible, most fully in the writings of Saint Paul of Tarsus (e.g., "For why should my liberty be determined by someone else's conscience?").[175] In the apostle's letter to the Romans, written around 55 A.D., he discusses how Christians should deal with other Christians who hold different beliefs. He notes that it is important not to judge others' consciences in debatable matters.[176]

Greek philosophers Plato and Socrates discussed freedom of thought minimally. Later, in the third century A.D., Greek and Roman thinkers developed the idea that individuals have a right to think for themselves and make decisions based on their judgment rather than submitting to authority figures. This idea finds expression in Christian thinkers like Origen of Alexandria, who insisted that

God gave individuals free will to make their own choices, and on the absolute freedom of each and every soul.[177-178] In later European tradition, major proponents include Themistius, Michel de Montaigne, Baruch Spinoza, John Locke, Voltaire, Alexandre Vinet, John Stuart Mill, and theologians like Samuel Rutherford and others.

Thanks to this legacy in the West, we have enjoyed many freedoms: freedom from censorship, freedom from religious persecution, and even freedom from discrimination. Many argue that these freedoms tend to vanish over time due to increased globalization and top-down impositions from governments. Article 18 of the United Nations Declaration of Human Rights,[179] about this freedom is a reminder: "Everyone has the right to freedom of thought, conscience and religion." Freedom of thought is the right to form opinions independently and express them freely. Freedom of expression is the right to communicate those opinions in any manner and by any means. "Shouting fire in a crowded theater"[180] is a famous phrase to illustrate legal limits; in this case, using speech or actions made for the principal purpose of creating panic are appropriately prohibited by law.

The right to freedom of expression is one of the most fundamental rights, and freedom of expression and thought are the cornerstones of democracy. To govern ourselves, we need to have the ability to express ourselves and think freely about our government. Censorship is the enemy of freedom, and it limits our ability to think critically and our ability to decide for ourselves what's true and what's false.

In a world where information is power, it's vital to ensure that everyone has access to as many truthful sources as possible. And that is why we need to protect freedom of expression—the best way for people to get their hands on accurate facts is by letting them say whatever they want about those facts. It is more important than ever before that we educate our children to understand the importance of the liberties we have enjoyed historically but that we cannot take for granted.

Freedom of Religion

Freedom of religion is a vital part of the human experience. It can be challenging to promote religious freedom everywhere in the world, but we should try. The idea of religious liberty has a long history, starting with Classical and Judeo-Christian traditions that encouraged religious tolerance. However, it wasn't until the Reformation that religious freedom became a major social and political issue. Over the past two centuries, the idea of religious liberty has advanced and has found diverse forms of political expression. Sadly, today millions are persecuted worldwide because of their religious beliefs.

Freedom of religion is at the heart of human liberty, and it has been—at the very least—recognized by most nations. Unfortunately, many people cannot exercise this fundamental liberty despite widespread recognition. But this is not different from many other freedoms; when we are free to choose, we are accountable for our choices. When we are responsible for our decisions, we will likely decide more wisely than when someone else makes those decisions—be it government or someone other than ourselves.

Freedom of religion is one of the most important rights we enjoy in Canada and the United States. This freedom is rooted deep in our history; it has been an integral part of our culture. But today, many people misunderstand the role that religion plays in our societies. For example, many people think that the "separation of church and state" means that we should exclude religion from public life and institutions like public schools. That is incorrect; the history of this concept in America exemplifies what historically has been a successful approach in this area. Thomas Jefferson wanted to protect states' freedom of religion from federal government control and facilitate the space to tend to their internal matters of faith and practice without government interference in general. The idea was not to privatize and minimize the impact of religion in society but, on the contrary, to create a situation conducive to the free practice of religion.[181]

Instruction

Who needs history when you can have a fun time learning about the history of education throughout civilizations? Briefly, the history of World civilizations [182,183] started in the Middle East about 3000 BC, whereas the North China civilization began around 1500 BC. The Mesopotamian and Egyptian civilizations flourished almost simultaneously during the first phase (3000–1500 BC). Sumerians developed the earliest known writing around 3100 BC, and scripture soon spread throughout other areas of Mesopotamia. The Egyptians invented hieroglyphics for this purpose, while Greeks, Romans; Indians; Persians; and Arabs later developed their alphabets. Common to ancient civilizations is their monumental literary achievement. The need for the continuity of these civilizations and their achievements made writing and some form of formal education indispensable.

The second phase of civilization began with the rise of Greek city-states around 750 BC. The Greeks established an urban culture that fostered intellectual inquiry and literary creativity. They also founded formal institutions of learning that included schools of philosophy, rhetoric, mathematics, and science. In ancient Greece, schools were mainly private, and people learned at home or by listening to recitations of poetry or plays by great writers. Imagine

Homer or Aeschylus in this role. Public schools also educated young men by reading books on mathematics and philosophy aloud.

The great philosophers of the day, such as Socrates, Plato, and Aristotle, were known for their contributions to education. Let us just mention a few examples. Socrates started the tradition of questioning accepted beliefs through reasoning and logic, and he believed in the value of right thinking and self-reflection.[184] Plato developed Socrates' ideas further and introduced the concept of a superior realm of abstract forms.

To illustrate the true nature of reality and the importance of knowledge, Plato describes the allegory of a cave.[185] He intended to compare "the effect of education and the lack of it on our nature." The young men are chained in a cave and only see shadows projected on the wall behind them, and they mistake these shadows for reality and call them "real things." Suppose they could see the actual World beyond that; they would realize the existence of real people, animals, trees, and the sky. Are our children trained to remain in the cave without access to a broader reality, prisoners of modern ideologies and interests?

Aristotle[186] added numerous contributions concerning education as an integral activity; he proposed that students learn by listening or reading and doing physical activities like sports or playing musical instruments. Regarding biology, Aristotle was the first person to study it systematically.[187] Greek philosophers contributed immeasurably to the development of future ideas throughout the Middle Ages up to this day.

It's no surprise that Christian institutions would be the first to establish schools and universities. After all, Jesus was a teacher, and He instructed in the ways of God. But it's not just that—Christianity is fundamentally about spiritual transformation and education (the word "catechism" comes from the Greek for "instruction by word of mouth"). By the twelfth century, education expanded explosively.

That's when we got universities—and a whole new world of learning with them. The first universities [188,189] started in Bologna and Paris, but Oxford and Cambridge soon followed suit. Then came Rome, Naples, Salamanca, Seville, Prague, Vienna, Cologne, Heidelberg, and the list continues! There were 62 recognized universities in Europe by 1500! The university was a novel phenomenon in European history, which developed and matured at the heart of Christian Europe. Nothing like it had existed in Greece or Rome. These new institutions provided space both theological and secular so that they could teach scientific knowledge alongside theological matters.

The term "scientific" derives from "scientia" in Latin, meaning knowledge applicable to any field of expertise, including botany, mathematics, or even theology. Monasteries were houses for monks and priests to test their strength of faith by secluding themselves from the World. These monks were not only in search of God but also searched for answers to questions about science. Many monks were scholars and manuscript writers, and artists. Monasteries were centers for scientific research because of the monks' level of education and understanding of various scientific fields.

It is fair to say that Christianity was at the forefront of nearly every major innovation in scientific history. Both Christianity and science aim at understanding things rationally, clearly, and carefully. Historians and Medieval scholars Lynn White (Medieval Technology and Social Change)[190] and Jean Gimpel[191] (The medieval machine: the industrial revolution of the Middle Ages) described the technological revolution as unlike anything known in classical times. Dinesh D'Souza quoted them in his book "What's So Great About Christianity."[192] Both historians describe how the agricultural techniques of the monasteries; theoretical and experimental study of the universities propelled Europe to develop a new way of understanding nature and making it work for mere mortals. As a result, a new society emerged with schools, farms, and workshops, taking learning and agricultural production to a new level. Inventions of the period included, among others, the waterwheel, the windmill, the chimney, paper money, eyeglasses, the mechanical clock, and public libraries. Though humble as they may seem, these and other innovations would transform the World.

In the sixteenth century, an event known as the Reformation changed the course of history.[193] It brought major changes to how we see our world. It introduced a new idea: knowledge belongs to us all, especially when it comes to matters of conscience each person should have the freedom to decide. Preparing the way, in 1436 John Gutenberg had invented the movable-type printing press. The first book ever printed this way was the Bible, the foundational book of Western Civilization. Protestants believe that through Christ, they have been given direct access to God, just like a priest; thus, the doctrine is called the priesthood of all believers, which was a powerful notion. The early Protestants didn't know it, but they were providing a theological foundation that would help propel Europe's emerging scientific culture with great vitality.

If you're a Christian, you probably already know that Christianity was one of the most important forces behind the birth of modern science.[194-195] But just in case you need a refresher to share with your child, here's a quick rundown of some of the great scientists who were also Christians: Copernicus, Kepler, Francis Bacon (a philosopher considered the father of the scientific method), Galileo, Brahe, Descartes, Boyle, Newton, Leibniz, Gassendi, Pascal, Mersenne, Cuvier, Harvey, Dalton, Faraday, Herschel, Joule, Lyell, Lavoisier, Priestley, Kelvin, Ohm, Ampere, Steno, Pasteur, Maxwell, Planck, Mendel. Some of these scientists, including Gassendi, Mersenne, and Georges Lemaitre—the Belgian astronomer who first proposed the "big bang" theory for the origin of the Universe—were clergymen. Mendel, whose discovery of the principles of heredity, was a monk. This list goes on and on—and it includes some of the most influential names in history. In more contemporary times, there is also a very long list of Jewish scientists and thinkers whose contributions are immense.[196] Many are atheists, but the theists did not see a contradiction between science and faith.

Is there compatibility between faith and reason? Are these two forms of knowledge necessary? For your answer, these are your people! Modern science was carried forward on the shoulders of those giants. Some were Protestant, and some were Catholic, but none saw a contradiction between science and their faith. The founders of modern science insisted that their work was "for the glory of God." For them, science was a profoundly theological project.

There were undoubtedly similar circumstances in other continents and cultures, but historians of science tell us that science could only develop in the West. It originated from a way of thinking that was deeply Christian in its presuppositions. God made us after His image means—among other things—we can understand the Creator's handiwork. The intelligibility of nature means that it exhibits an orderly structure and patterning; this allowed for empirical investigation into nature. "The reason within matches the reason without" is a phrase attributed to the late John Polkinghorne—renowned quantum physicist and theologian who had a distinguished career as a physicist at Cambridge University. He also said: "When you realize that the laws of nature must be incredibly finely tuned to produce the universe we see, that conspires to plant the idea that the universe did not just happen, but that there must be a purpose behind it."[197] Charles Townes, who shared the 1964 Nobel Prize in Physics for discovering the principles of the laser, observed: "Many have a feeling that somehow intelligence must have been involved in the laws of the universe."[198]

The contingency of nature showed that nature requires a creator, it is not an eternal self-existing universe, and God could have created it differently. Man's fallibility implies that we cannot fully trust ourselves or our senses to discover the world around us, even if our faculties were not distorted by sin. Human beings are fallible and biased, hence the need for a (scientific) method for correction. Underlying these presuppositions was also the idea that natural knowledge should lead us to reverence and good stewardship rather than relentless exploitation and control over nature. This distinctive worldview also motivated much subsequent scientific inquiry; for example, the search for underlying order led to a discovery of the laws of nature.

Why Is This Important for Your Child?

You may have heard it said that Christianity and science are antithetical, incompatible, or scientific findings disproved God. Your child may be learning this view at school or in other places. Nowadays, it is fashionable for educators (atheist teachers) to make extreme claims about the alleged incompatibility between Christianity and science. In a survey by Pew Research, many respondents mention that "science" is why they do not believe in religious teachings.[199] They said, "I'm a scientist now, and I don't believe in miracles," while others reference "common sense," "logic," or a "lack of evidence." Others say they do not believe in God. Don't be fooled. History teaches us that Christians have been great scientists who have used their scientific skills to investigate the world they live in and glorify God through their discoveries.

The materialist worldview that dominates our culture today does not want us to believe there is more than meets the eye. From the miracles of Jesus to the miracle of your own life, there's a wealth of captivating information that isn't taught in school—it doesn't fit in the materialist Worldview. It's enchanting, genuine, and if we pay attention, often profound insights come from top scientists, educators, and historians. Ignored by mainstream academia and public school are many areas that represent a wealth of valuable, worldview-changing information. A few examples are archaeological discoveries,[200] the Shroud of Turin,[201,202] research on near-death experiences (scientific literature, not anecdotal cases),[203-205] the nature of biological information and life,[206] the mind, soul, and the reality of God.

The Bible is essential in any educated person's library—but it's more than just a good read. It is the foundational Book of our civilization. Jordan Peterson is a Canadian psychologist, YouTube personality, author, and professor emeritus at the University of Toronto. Jordan Peterson is not a confessed believer, but he looks at the Bible and says: "It's not that the Bible is true. It's that the Bible is the prerequisite for the manifestation of truth, which makes it far more true than just 'true.' It's a whole different kind of truth. And I think that's not just literally the case—in fact—I think it can't be otherwise. This is the only way to solve the problem of perception."[207] Dig deep and discover the treasure for you and your children. The following are but a few examples of hot topics in contemporary science and history that your children should know according to their level; in contrast with some materialistic concepts, they may learn in school.

In the Beginning, God

One after the other, the discoveries of contemporary science point towards a transcendent reality. It has been confirming a truth familiar to us for thousands of years. One of the most astonishing scientific facts about the Universe is? It started from literally nothing. How does something come from nothing? And what could have caused that first "big bang" that started everything, as science confirms? It sounds like a question you may have asked yourself as a child. What precisely can we know about the cause of our Universe? Here theologians and philosophers come to our help.[208] A cause of energy, matter, and space and time cannot be material itself. After all, it caused the material world into being. This cause must be uncaused, timeless, and spaceless with no beginning or end. This cause must also be personal and invested with freedom of will to decide to create and must possess tremendous power. How can we summarize all these attributes? In one word: God. But God has revealed more about himself; more on that later.

The Origin of Life on Earth

The origin of life on Earth is a question that has baffled scientists for many decades. It is one of the great mysteries of science. So how did we get from energy, matter, and space-time to life? Where is the evidence for the idea that life originated naturally? In other words, how do you get life from non-life? This question is beyond physics, chemistry, and biology – it brings in a fourth area: the realm of information science. Information science governs living organisms, including their internal structures and external expressions of life, such as animal behavior and plant growth habits. In nature, we find patterns but not specified information. In contrast, we see the most complex and multilayered patterns of information of all in living things.

If you are walking on the beach and find a phrase on the sand: "David loves Mary!" you immediately know two things. First, that is a message that natural processes like the waves or something of that nature did not create. Second, there is a mind behind it. If you accept the materialist worldview for the origin of life, you need to postulate a case of a something-from-nothing leap of faith! In a concise presentation, the late Frank Pastore[209]—a former major league baseball pitcher and popular radio talk show host with several academic degrees—referred to these materialistic jumps as big bangs or something-from-nothing jumps. You can use this type of brief visual presentation (5:29 minutes) for discussion with your teenage child.

Chances are you've heard of DNA as the genetic material in our cells that contains our genes. But how many times have you thought about what this looks like? Your DNA is made of tiny twigs, the famous double-helix of DNA but if you stretched them all out, they would be 67 billion miles long—enough to reach the Moon and back 150,000 times. [210] If stretched out, the DNA from one cell would be six feet long. The human genome is about 3.2 billion letters of DNA code—more than 98 percent of which is noncoding.[210] This DNA still plays an essential role in how our cells function, but not by coding proteins. They operate like the invisible hand of an orchestra director telling what genes should be playing (active) and which one should not. These genes used to be called "junk" DNA but not anymore. And embedded in that DNA is a four-letter chemical alphabet that spells the precise assembly instructions for every protein in your body. Just as the English language uses a 26-letter alphabet, this uses a 4-letter chemical alphabet.

According to Bill Gates, founder of Microsoft Corporation, "Biological information is the most important information we can discover, because over the next several decades it will revolutionize medicine. Human DNA is like a computer program but far, far more advanced than any software ever created."[211] Last year in an article published in Nature[212]—the British weekly scientific journal—the authors wrote about the characteristics of DNA and its high information density. The information capacity is nearly 455 billion GB of data per gram. But that is not all; DNA provides a host of other unique potential advantages:

1) Highly parallel computation within the storage system itself.

2) Low energy requirements and rapid high-capacity transportation of data.

3) Potentially longer lifetimes—and stability of decades or centuries compared to conventional media.

Think of it: such fantastic stability and capacity of information originated in the very tiny nucleus of a microscopic cell. I can't but think about an intelligent signature!

The genetic code is an older and more elaborate form of information storage than anything we have invented. It stores vital information needed to create and maintain every living species in incredible detail. The code contains instructions about how cells work, how they interact with each other, and what reactions occur when they do so. All these point towards a mind, a super-intelligence. By the way, the next disruption could be in the World of synthetic DNA data storage. DNA has a very high information density capacity plus excellent stability. And no, this is not science fiction; projections indicate that the global DNA Data Storage market size will reach multi-million by 2028.[213]

We find information at the foundation of life. What is its origin? Could information arise from non-intelligent causes? Whenever we find information and trace it back to its source, we always find a mind. Astrophysicists look for informational patterns in radio signals; it would signify extraterrestrial intelligent life. Whether we look at a hieroglyphic inscription or a phrase written on the sand, it always points to a mind.

Beneath the surface of our skin lies a microcosm of super tiny molecular machines (nanomachines). Engineers recognize them as marvels of design and efficiency. Their integration is so that only if they function together can a cell work properly: without them, death occurs. Scientists have found molecular machines in everything from bacteria to humans, including photosynthesis! A biological molecule can achieve its function only when it is in a highly specific form. Components in a cell are themselves the embodiment of highly specified information as much as the DNA molecule that provides the blueprint for their synthesis. We have no plausible naturalistic explanation for the origin of life. Leading researchers in the field of chemical evolutionary theory acknowledge this.

Francis Crick, the co-discoverer of the structure of DNA, admitted: "the chances that the long polymer molecules that vitally sustain all living things, both proteins and DNA, could have been assembled by random processes from the chemical units of which they are made are so small as to be negligible."[214] Nalin Chandra Wickramasinghe is a Sri Lankan-born British mathematician, astronomer, and astrobiologist. He stated in an interview: "From my earliest training as a scientist, I was very strongly brainwashed to believe that science cannot be consistent with any kind of deliberate creation. That notion has had to be painfully shed. At the moment, I can't find any rational argument to knock down the view which argues for conversion to God. We used to have an open mind; now we realize that the only logical answer to life is creation-and not accidental random shuffling."[215] James Tour is a leading scientist at Rice University in Houston with many accomplishments and awards. He is blunt: "Scientists are Clueless on the Origin of Life."[216] Paul Davies is an English physicist and writer who researches in the areas of theoretical physics, cosmology, and astrobiology. In his book "The Fifth Miracle: The Search for the Origin and Meaning of Life" says: "Many investigators feel uneasy stating in public that the origin of life is a mystery, even though behind closed doors they admit they are baffled. There are two reasons for their unease. First, they feel it opens the door to religious fundamentalism... Second, they worry that a frank admission of ignorance will undermine funding."[217]

The Language of Mathematics

The language of mathematics, rightly viewed, possesses not only truth but a special form of beauty—a beauty austere, like that of sculpture, and deep like profound spiritual reality. It is said that nature has been written in this language. A true spirit of delight, exaltation, and a sense of being more than a physical object, the touchstone of the highest excellence, is to be found in mathematics as surely as poetry. Again, "the reason within matches the reason without."

The force of this truth compelled Eugene Paul Wigner—a Hungarian American physicist, Nobel Prize in Physics in 1963, not a believer himself—to write in a famous article: "The miracle of the appropriateness of the language of mathematics for the formulation of the laws of physics is a wonderful gift which we neither understand nor deserve. We should be grateful for it and hope that it will remain valid in future research and that it will extend, for better or for worse, to our pleasure, even though perhaps also to our bafflement, to wide branches of learning."[218]

The Origin of Consciousness

"How can mere matter originate consciousness?" Atheist Colin McGinn asks, "How can mere matter originate consciousness? How did evolution convert the water of biological tissue into the wine of consciousness? Consciousness seems like a radical novelty in the universe, not prefigured by the aftereffects of the Big Bang; so how did it contrive to spring into being from what preceded it?"[219] What a leap for the mind! It's like looking at the stunning gallery of art in the Louvre and deciding that it all came from a box of crayons with no artist behind it! Or listening to Beethoven's Fifth Symphony and concluding: it just arose by chance in a particular key and tempo!

If we are simply products of random processes and natural selection, where did our "self" originate? The West has always wanted to establish a link between matter and consciousness. In the predominant view in the tradition, consciousness is the logical consequence of there being a mind in the beginning. The magnificent prologue to the Gospel of St. John begins: "In the beginning was the Word"[220] (Logos). Many things point to the existence of the soul, from the fact that we have consciousness to the belief that we can have free will!

The brain is an anatomical organ essential for this life, but there's more to us than just our brains. The mind is not just an emergent property of biology or neurons in the brain. At the core of our being, more than just a brain is a soul. It is immaterial and indivisible. Something may hide, but it may still be there. It seems like the soul would be invisible, depending on how you think. However, if we were to think of the soul as something that makes us who we are, then it also seems like we could perceive it somehow. Think of this as an example of a different kind of perception (a form of metacognition, if you will).

Even though you can't see your mind (which is hidden), you know that you have one because you have thoughts and understand things. However immaterial, the soul participates in the World through your body. First, the soul engages in the development and growth of the organism from the beginning. Note that the whole comes first and then the parts. The soul cooperates in animating the body "as a whole" and endows us with the faculty of consciousness—in cooperation with the brain. We are a uni-totality of spirit, soul, and body.

There is nothing inherently wrong in positing something not directly observable to explain something we cannot see. The question is whether such a proposition provides genuine explanatory power and is consistent with the evidence. The soul is invisible and known only by its effects. And indeed, many things are invisible, such as thoughts, love, and gravity, and we know them only through our experience and their impact on us and the world around us. The soul is akin to that: it is an actual reality, more significant than many of us can see. The soul is extended in space with every perception and manifested intimately in every introspection, our inner thoughts. In many ways, the soul is equivalent to being alive. It is a blueprint for the innermost dynamic configuration of our bodies—close though not identical to our concept of information—and the source of our consciousness. The spirit is a faculty of our souls. In a word, the soul unifies us as persons, both physically and mentally! This concept of the soul is in complete opposition to the notion of the soul as a phantasmagorical, ethereal vapor or essence. It also opposes the materialist idea that we are merely biological machines functioning only on mechanistic principles.

The End of Materialism

"Secularism is a belief system that rejects religion, or the belief that religion should not be part of the affairs of the state or part of public education."[221] The word secular comes from the Latin word saeculum, which means century. While there are various ways to define secularism, the simplest definition is that it is a system that exists without religion. Such an idea permeates every aspect of our Western societies; this is called secularization. The foundation of the process of secularization is philosophical materialism. But materialism is exhausting its course, and secularism is waning.

The recent declination of Darwin, Marx, and Freud as the prophets of the secular world can be interpreted as part of a reconsideration of traditional values and realities such as God, faith, and the soul. Darwin's contribution to science was significant, but it's crumbling as a pillar sustaining a materialist worldview and a myth of origins. Marx offered a Utopian vision of society, but the disastrous fruits of his experiment have been evident if only we had eyes to see. Freud's theories have been rejected for the most part, and his method of dealing with guilt has failed. They were centered on pathology and biology, ignoring the spiritual dimension of the human person. Add to this the current critique from neuroscience. But beware! Today new prophets linger at the top, and they propose a Godless World in the name of science and technology. In addition to the difficulties we have already mentioned, such a worldview faces challenges in various areas of science.

The observer's problem[222] confronts quantum physics; reality appears to require consciousness, even a "cosmic observer" to function. For the World to unfold with its multiple levels of intertwined patterns it requires encoded intelligence. Biology also presents innumerable problems, including the origin of information in living organisms, the issue of complexity, and the challenges presented by the emergence of new levels of organization with radically new properties. Many Biologists accept that we cannot explain living organisms in mechanistic terms. Fred Hoyle, the English astronomer, summarized it well: "A commonsense interpretation of the facts suggests that a superintellect has monkeyed with physics, as well as with chemistry and biology, and that there are no blind forces worth speaking about in nature. The numbers one calculates from the facts seem to me so overwhelming as to put this conclusion almost beyond question." [223]

Beyond physics, chemistry, and biology, we find what philosophers of neuroscience consider "the hard problem of consciousness"[224] an insurmountable challenge for the materialist. Admittedly, methodological materialism in science had been fruitful, but now it has become an impediment to development in many areas. The current dominance of materialism in the academic world has stifled the research based on nonmaterialistic ideas in science and hindered the investigation of the mind, consciousness, memory, and life. The legacy of materialism has also left us with a poor and hopeless conception of who we are.

Transcendence

Transcendence points to the highest good. As commonly understood by philosophers, the transcendentals are the properties of being that give all things their value. Being itself, truth, love, justice, and beauty are among them. The transcendentals represent what we seek in our lives and what makes life worth living. A long history in the philosophy of Western Civilization deals with these ideas. Transcendence inspires in us the desire to enter a higher state of being, a deep relationship with God. It is a source of aspiration to bring good into the World and make it better, beautiful, and happier. Christianity brought a powerful unification; it dared to affirm that these values point to God, but it sustains that God became a man in whom these values embodied. Other traditions claim that humans may climb to divine heights or become God. Only Christianity claims that God became man to take upon himself the suffering of humanity and offer redemption and eternal life if we accept this act of divine grace through an act of trust and faith.

It is a historical irony that today your child may not be taught in many schools about the life of the man at the heart of Western Civilization. I respectfully plead with you to teach your child about the Way to all that is Good, Just, Beautiful, and True. The contrasting greatness and humility of this one man that transforms the World are beautifully captured in the poem attributed to James Allen Francis:

"One Solitary Life

He was born in an obscure village, the child of a peasant. He grew up in another village, where he worked in a carpenter shop until he was 30. Then, for three years, he was an itinerant preacher.

He never wrote a book. He never held an office. He never had a family or owned a home. He didn't go to college. He never lived in a big city. He never traveled 200 miles from the place where he was born. He did none of the things that usually accompany greatness. He had no credentials but himself.

He was only 33 when the tide of public opinion turned against him. His friends ran away. One of them denied him. He was turned over to his enemies and went through the mockery of a trial. He was nailed to a cross between two thieves. While he was dying, his executioners gambled for his garments, the only property he had on Earth. When he was dead, he was laid in a borrowed grave, through the pity of a friend.

Twenty centuries have come and gone, and today he is the central figure of the human race. I am well within the mark when I say that all the armies that ever marched, all the navies that ever sailed, all the parliaments that ever sat, all the kings that ever reigned--put together--have not affected the life of man on this Earth as much as that one, solitary life."[225]

Many historians would consider Jesus of Nazareth the most influential person in history, and the events surrounding his death and resurrection are essential to this understanding. While many believe in the resurrection of Jesus Christ, most would say that they believe it just by faith—nothing wrong with that; it is life-changing. However, most people are unaware that most New Testament scholars and historians have come to agree on the central facts about the events following Jesus' crucifixion.[226-230] These facts are:

1. His death by crucifixion

2. His appearances to his disciples after his death

3. The empty tomb

4. And the origin of the disciples' belief that he had risen from the dead

In fact, over the last decades, a remarkable transformation in understanding these extraordinary historical facts has occurred. Without any plausible naturalistic explanation, the burden of proof is not on the believer but on the skeptics. I would like you to ponder these words from C. S. Lewis: "Christianity, if false, is of no importance, and if true, of infinite importance. The only thing it cannot be is moderately important."[231]

If you need the motivation to be yourself in a position to inspire your child, you are in good company. I have a quote from one extraordinary author. G. K. Chesterton's reply was simple and profound when asked, "What's wrong with the world today?" "Dear Sir, I am."[232] A new world emerges when we genuinely overcome the old self and are transformed.

St. Thomas Aquinas warned that wealth, pleasure, power, and honor are the four typical substitutes for God.[167] These four things appear to be the most valuable goods of life and represent value. Sensing the void within, we attempt to fill it up with some combination of them—but only by letting God fill us up can we do so. St. Augustine of Hippo's phrase from his "Confessions" resonates with all thirsty hearts throughout the centuries: "Thou hast made us for thyself, O Lord, and our heart is restless until it finds its rest in thee."[233] In the famous hymn Amazing Grace, we hear: "I once was lost, but now I am found, was blind, but now I see." In the words of C. S. Lewis: "I believe in Christianity as I believe that the Sun has risen, not only because I see it but because by it, I see everything else."[234]

Where does the word "education" come from? It comes from the Latin word "Educare" which means "to lead or draw out" and 'to bring forth'. The child's innate gifts should be appropriately cared for and given scope to grow and develop. The most important aspect of education is not processing information, learning skills, or memorizing facts but rather forming a virtuous soul, which leads to an ethical society. Education needs to center on character development. In the words of José Martí: "It is necessary to make virtue fashionable" and "Talent is a gift that brings with it an obligation to serve the world, and not ourselves, for it is not of our making."[235] Mountains culminate in peaks and civilization in one man, the Nazarene. At the summit of civilization, Jesus of Nazareth incarnates redemption, divine love, positive discipline, glorious freedom, and instruction that profits in this and the life to come—the cornerstone we would be wise to use for our foundation. In the Christian understanding, the ground of all reality is one God and at the same time, a divine family, Father, Son, and Holy Spirit. In the inexhaustible view of Jesus Christ, we can see a synthesis of divine love, discipline, freedom, instruction, and a truthful and coherent Worldview.

AFTERWORD

I salute you for your commitment to providing the best foundation possible for your child's education. The first years in children's lives are the most important in developing the foundation for their future. Your practice of love, discipline, and freedom with your children will define them and mold them into good citizens of society who will make the future better by their actions. This book's unity derives from a rock-solid understanding that children benefit the most when shaped by the power of love, discipline, and instruction to live lives of freedom and joy supported by a coherent, time-tested worldview.

Each chapter in this book helps sustain the structure upon which you can build the house, creating the space for developing a happy, healthy, and resilient personality in your child. The principles are intertwined; they reinforce each other. They can make the arduous task ahead more manageable with the hope that the effort will be amply rewarding. All parents agree on one thing: parenting a child is not easy. There are many challenges: endless "why" questions, sleep deprivation, public tantrums, and more. However, any parent needs to remember that their child is a gift from God, a joy, and a responsibility.

By clearly understanding the central pillars, you can focus on the practical tips and various applications around them with better

· AFTERWORD ·

consistency and efficacy. The principles are so simple and profound; they will help you find something new to apply in your daily life as a parent! In this era of overwhelming information availability, defining the priorities for your parental strategy is more challenging and necessary than it used to be in previous generations. Love, Discipline, Freedom, Instruction, and a sound Worldview are principles to live by from the early years and then for the rest of your children's lives. These basic concepts will remain an enduring guide for your children to live well as adults. These principles' beauty is the natural continuity that allows for ongoing growth in those areas well into mature adulthood. Your children will be to the culture salt—that preserves and flavors—and light that exposes, illuminates, and guides. They will help create in your family a culture that could live on from generation to generation.

REFERENCES

About the Author

a. García OD, Machado C, Román JM, Cabrera A, Díaz-Comas L, Rivera B, Grave de Peralta R. Heart rate variability in coma and brain death. In: Machado C, editor. Brain death (proceedings of the Second International Symposium on Brain Death). Development in neurology, vol. 9. Amsterdam: Elsevier; 1995. p. 191–200.

b. Machado C, García OD, Gutiérrez J, Portela L, García MC. Heart rate variability in comatose and brain-dead patients. Clin Neurophysiol 2005; 116:2859–60.

Introduction

1. Source: https://www.ncbi.nlm.nih.gov/pmc/articles/PMC3330161/

2. Source:https://www.psychologytoday.com/us/blog/the-asymmetric-brain/202106/what-age-does-mental-illness-begin

3. Source:https://www.canada.ca/en/public-health/services/publications/healthy-living/suicide-canada-key-statistics-infographic.html

4. Source:https://www.cdc.gov/suicide/facts/disparities-in-suicide.html

5. Source:https://www.cdc.gov/nchs/products/databriefs/db56.htm

6. Source:https://www.cdc.gov/nchs/data/hestat/obesity-child-17-18/obesity-child.htm

7. Source:https://digital.newint.com.au/issues/110/articles/2665

8. Source:https://www.psychologytoday.com/us/blog/talking-about-men/201707/is-increase-in-individualism-damaging-our-mental-health

9. Source:https://www.census.gov/library/publications/2018/demo/p60-262.html

10. https://www.cdc.gov/childrensmentalhealth/data.html

Chapter One - Love

11. Lewis, C.S. God in the Dock. William B. Eerdmans Publishing Company, Grand Rapids. 1970. p. 49.

12. Scripture taken from the New King James Version®. Copyright © 1982 by Thomas Nelson. Used by permission. All rights reserved.

13. Lewis, C. S. The Four Loves. New York, Harcourt, Brace [1960].

14. J. Cooper and D.S. Hutchinson (edd.), Plato: Complete Works. Indianapolis: Hackett Publishing Company, 1997.

15. Source:https://archive.org/details/completeworks00plat/page/n7/mode/2up

16. W. D. Ross, Aristotle(1923) https://archive.org/details/in.ernet.dli.2015.536932

17. Source:https://46y5eh11fhgw3ve3ytpwxt9r-wpengine.netdna-ssl.com/wp-content/uploads/2019/02/EpigeneticsInfographic_FINAL.pdf

18. Source:https://www.nature.com/articles/s42003-021-02316-6

19. Source:https://www.biographyonline.net/music/mozart.html#:~:text=Wolfgang%20Amadeus%20Mozart%20%2827%20January%201756%20%E2%80%93%205,pieces%20of%20symphonic%2C%20chamber%2C%20operatic%2C%20and%20choral%20music.

20. Source: https://www.liveabout.com/wolfgang-amadeus-mozart-child-prodigy-723779

21. Report to the Royal Society about Mozart https://royalsocietypublishing.org/doi/epdf/10.1098/rstl.1770.0008

22. Source: https://www.radcliffe.harvard.edu/schlesinger-library/collections/helen-keller

23. Helen Keller. (1903) The Story of my Life. Source: https://archive.org/details/storyofmylife0000kell/page/n15/mode/2up

24. Source: https://en.wikipedia.org/wiki/Jos%C3%A9_Ra%C3%BAl_CapablancaCapablanca article by Munsey's Magazine, October 1916, pages 94-96.

25. Source: https://www.chesshistory.com/winter/extra/capablanca4.html

26. Source:https://pubmed.ncbi.nlm.nih.gov/30396119/

27. Source: https://hfh.fas.harvard.edu/parental-warmth

28. Maselko J, Kubzansky L, Lipsitt L, Buka SL. Mother's affection at 8 months predicts emotional distress in adulthood. J Epidemiol Community Health. 2011 Jul;65(7):621-5. doi: 10.1136/jech.2009.097873. Epub 2010 Jul 26. PMID: 20660942; PMCID: PMC3118641.

29. Mäntymaa M, Puura K, Luoma I, Latva R, Salmelin RK, Tamminen T. Shared pleasure in early mother-infant interaction: predicting lower levels of emotional and behavioral problems in the child and protecting against the influence of parental psychopathology. Infant Ment Health J. 2015 Mar-Apr;36(2):223-37. doi: 10.1002/imhj.21505. Epub 2015 Mar 4. PMID: 25739800.

30. Francis AJ. Mother's affection at 8 months predicts emotional distress in adulthood: errors in interpretation. J Epidemiol Community Health. 2011 Apr;65(4):384. doi: 10.1136/jech.2010.122804. Epub 2010 Dec 3. PMID: 21131302.

31. Source: https://www.science.org/content/article/two-psychologists-followed-1000-new-zealanders-decades-here-s-what-they-found-about-how?cookieSet=1

32. Source: https://today.duke.edu/2021/01/self-controlled-children-tend-be-healthier-middle-aged-adults New Zealand

33. Sharma SR, Gonda X, Dome P, Tarazi FI. What's Love Got to do with it: Role of oxytocin in trauma, attachment and resilience. Pharmacol Ther. 2020 Oct;214:107602. doi: 10.1016/j.pharmthera.2020.107602. Epub 2020 Jun 6. PMID: 32512017.

34. Carter CS, Kenkel WM, MacLean EL, Wilson SR, Perkeybile AM, Yee JR, Ferris CF, Nazarloo HP, Porges SW, Davis JM, Connelly JJ, Kingsbury MA. Is Oxytocin "Nature's Medicine"? Pharmacol Rev. 2020 Oct;72(4):829-861. doi: 10.1124/pr.120.019398. PMID: 32912963; PMCID: PMC7495339.

35. Source: https://obgyn.onlinelibrary.wiley.com/doi/10.1111/jog.15023

36. King CE, Gano A, Becker HC. The role of oxytocin in alcohol and drug abuse. Brain Res. 2020 Jun 1;1736:146761. doi: 10.1016/j.brainres.2020.146761. Epub 2020 Mar 3. PMID: 32142721; PMCID: PMC7137097

37. Lee, Mary R et al. "Targeting the Oxytocin System to Treat Addictive Disorders: Rationale and Progress to Date." CNS drugs vol. 30,2 (2016): 109-23. doi:10.1007/s40263-016-0313-z.

38. McGregor IS, Bowen MT. Breaking the loop: oxytocin as a potential treatment for drug addiction. Horm Behav. 2012 Mar;61(3):331-9. doi: 10.1016/j.yhbeh.2011.12.001. Epub 2011 Dec 14. PMID: 22198308.

39. Edinoff AN, Thompson E, Merriman CE, et al. Oxytocin, a Novel Treatment for Methamphetamine Use Disorder. Neurol Int. 2022;14(1):186-198. Published 2022 Jan 30. doi:10.3390/neurolint14010015

40. King CE, Gano A, Becker HC. The role of oxytocin in alcohol and drug abuse. Brain Res. 2020;1736:146761. doi:10.1016/j.brainres.2020.146761

41. Mairesse J, Zinni M, Pansiot J, et al. Oxytocin receptor agonist reduces perinatal brain damage by targeting microglia. Glia. 2019;67(2):345-359. doi:10.1002/glia.23546

42. Brown CH, Grattan DR. Does maternal oxytocin protect the fetal brain?. Trends Endocrinol Metab. 2007;18(6):225-226. doi:10.1016/j.tem.2007.04.003

43. Wu Z, Xie C, Kuang H, et al. Oxytocin mediates neuroprotection against hypoxic-ischemic injury in hippocampal CA1 neuron of neonatal rats. Neuropharmacology. 2021;187:108488. doi:10.1016/j.neuropharm.2021.108488

44. Source: https://www.health.harvard.edu/mind-and-mood/oxytocin-the-love-hormone

45. Harwood-Gross A, Lambez B, Feldman R, Zagoory-Sharon O, Rassovsky Y. The Effect of Martial Arts Training on Cognitive and Psychological Functions in At-Risk Youths. Front Pediatr. 2021;9:707047. Published 2021 Oct 22. doi:10.3389/fped.2021.707047.

46. Harvey Alan R., Links Between the Neurobiology of Oxytocin and Human Musicality. Frontiers in Human Neuroscience. Vol. 14, 2020. Source: https://www.frontiersin.org/article/10.3389/fnhum.2020.00350 DOI=10.3389/fnhum.2020.00350

47. Morhenn, V., Beavin, L. E., & Zak, P. J. (2012). Massage increases oxytocin and reduces adrenocorticotropin hormone in humans. Alternative therapies in health and medicine, 18(6), 11–18.

48. Ionio C, Ciuffo G, Landoni M. Parent-Infant Skin-to-Skin Contact and Stress Regulation: A Systematic Review of the Literature. Int J Environ Res Public Health. 2021;18(9):4695. Published 2021 Apr 28. doi:10.3390/ijerph18094695

49. Kim, Eun Joo et al. "Stress effects on the hippocampus: a critical review." Learning & memory (Cold Spring Harbor, N.Y.) vol. 22,9 411-6. 18 Aug. 2015, doi:10.1101/lm.037291.114

50. Uvnäs-Moberg, Kerstin et al. "Self-soothing behaviors with particular reference to oxytocin release induced by non-noxious sensory stimulation." Frontiers in psychology vol. 5 1529. 12 Jan. 2015, doi:10.3389/fpsyg.2014.01529

51. Katherine Harmon. How Important Is Physical Contact with Your Infant? May 6, 2010 Source: https://www.scientificamerican.com/article/infant-touch/

52. Rogol A. D. (2020). Emotional Deprivation in Children: Growth Faltering and Reversible Hypopituitarism. Frontiers in endocrinology, 11, 596144. https://doi.org/10.3389/fendo.2020.596144

53. Narvaez, Darcia et al. "The importance of early life touch for psychosocial and moral development." Psicologia, reflexao e critica : revista semestral do Departamento de Psicologia da UFRGS vol. 32,1 16. 2 Aug. 2019, doi:10.1186/s41155-019-0129-0

54. Luby JL, Barch DM, Belden A, et al. Maternal support in early childhood predicts larger hippocampal volumes at school age. Proc Natl Acad Sci U S A. 2012;109(8):2854-2859. doi:10.1073/pnas.1118003109

55. Darcia Narvaez, et al. Extravagant Affection in Infancy Leads to Healthier, Happier, More Relational & Moral Adults. 2016 Source: https://www.patheos.com/blogs/faithonthecouch/2016/03/new-study-extravagant-affection-in-infancy-leads-to-healthier-happier-more-relational-moral-adults/

56. Judith E. Carroll, et al. Childhood abuse, parental warmth, and adult multisystem biological risk in the Coronary Artery Risk Development in Young Adults study. Contributed by Shelley E. Taylor, August 23, 2013 (sent for review July 16, 2013) 110 (42) 17149-17153 Source: https://doi.org/10.1073/pnas.1315458110.

57. Teicher MD. Wounds that time won't heal: the neurobiology of child abuse. Cerebrum: The Dana Forum on brain science. 2000;2:50–67.

58. Maselko, J et al. "Mother's affection at 8 months predicts emotional distress in adulthood." Journal of epidemiology and community health vol. 65,7 (2011): 621-5. doi:10.1136/jech.2009.097873

59. Cohen S, Janicki-Deverts D, Turner RB, Doyle WJ. Does hugging provide stress-buffering social support? A study of susceptibility to upper respiratory infection and illness. Psychol Sci. 2015;26(2):135-147. doi:10.1177/0956797614559284

60. Savage BM, Lujan HL, Thipparthi RR, DiCarlo SE. Humor, laughter, learning, and health! A brief review. Adv Physiol Educ. 2017;41(3):341-347. doi:10.1152/advan.00030.2017

61. Yim J. Therapeutic Benefits of Laughter in Mental Health: A Theoretical Review. Tohoku J Exp Med. 2016;239(3):243-249. doi:10.1620/tjem.239.243

62. Parenting by Play. Cooperative Extension Service Department of Family and Consumer Sciences.University of Wyoming. College of Agriculture Source: https://nc4h.ces.ncsu.edu/wp-content/uploads/2016/01/Wy1040.pdf?fwd=no

63. Lawrence J. Cohen. (2001) Playful Parenting. A Living Planet Book. Ballantine Books. New York.

64. Weisleder A, Fernald A. Talking to children matters: early language experience strengthens processing and builds vocabulary. Psychol Sci. 2013; 24(11):2143-2152. doi:10.1177/0956797613488145

65. Logan JAR, Justice LM, Yumuş M, Chaparro-Moreno LJ. When Children Are Not Read to at Home: The Million Word Gap. J Dev Behav Pediatr. 2019;40(5):383-386. doi:10.1097/DBP.0000000000000657

66. Reid Chassiakos YL, Radesky J, Christakis D, Moreno MA, Cross C; COUNCIL ON COMMUNICATIONS AND MEDIA. Children and Adolescents and Digital Media. Pediatrics. 2016;138(5):e20162593. doi:10.1542/peds.2016-2593

67. Bruce LD, Wu JS, Lustig SL, Russell DW, Nemecek DA. Loneliness in the United States: A 2018 National Panel Survey of Demographic, Structural, Cognitive, and Behavioral Characteristics. Am J Health Promot. 2019;33(8):1123-1133. doi:10.1177/0890117119856551

68. Holt-Lunstad J. Loneliness and Social Isolation as Risk Factors: The Power of Social Connection in Prevention. Am J Lifestyle Med. 2021;15(5):567-573. Published 2021 May 6. doi:10.1177/15598276211009454

69. Kelly ME, Duff H, Kelly S, et al. The impact of social activities, social networks, social support and social relationships on the cognitive functioning of healthy older adults: a systematic review. Syst Rev. 2017;6(1):259. Published 2017 Dec 19. doi:10.1186/s13643-017-0632-2

70. Umberson D, Montez JK. Social relationships and health: a flashpoint for health policy. J Health Soc Behav. 2010;51 Suppl(Suppl):S54-S66. doi:10.1177/0022146510383501

71. Strengthen relationships for longer, healthier life. January 18, 2011 Source: https://www.health.harvard.edu/healthbeat/strengthen-relationships-for-longer-healthier-life#:~:text=Dozens%20of%20studies%20have%20shown,well%20as%20with%20increased%20mortality.

72. The health benefits of strong relationships. Source: https://www.health.harvard.edu/staying-healthy/the-health-benefits-of-strong-relationships

73. Holt-Lunstad J, Smith TB, Layton JB. Social relationships and mortality risk: a meta-analytic review. PLoS Med. 2010;7(7):e1000316. Published 2010 Jul 27. doi:10.1371/journal.pmed.1000316

74. Friendships: Enrich your life and improve your health. Mayo Clinic Staff. Source: https://www.mayoclinic.org/healthy-lifestyle/adult-health/in-depth/friendships/art-20044860

75. Rowland L, Curry OS. A range of kindness activities boost happiness. J Soc Psychol. 2019;159(3):340-343. doi:10.1080/00224545.2018.1469461

76. American Heritage of the English Language. Source: https://ahdictionary.com/

77. David Schwartz. How Spending Quality Time Can Really Strengthen Families. Psychology Today. Posted February 7, 2021. Source: https://www.psychologytoday.com/ca/blog/adolescents-explained/202102/how-spending-quality-time-can-really-strengthen-families

78. Skeer MR, Ballard EL. Are family meals as good for youth as we think they are? A review of the literature on family meals as they pertain to adolescent risk prevention. J Youth Adolesc. 2013;42(7):943-963. doi:10.1007/s10964-013-9963-z

79. Verhage CL, Gillebaart M, van der Veek SMC, Vereijken CMJL. The relation between family meals and health of infants and toddlers: A review. Appetite. 2018;127:97-109. doi:10.1016/j.appet.2018.04.010

80. Harrison ME, Norris ML, Obeid N, Fu M, Weinstangel H, Sampson M. Systematic review of the effects of family meal frequency on psychosocial outcomes in youth. Can Fam Physician. 2015;61(2):e96-e106.

81. Source: https://www.health.harvard.edu/blog/home-cooking-healthy-family-meals-2018082114580#:~:text=Family%20meals%20are%20beneficial%20for,stress%20and%20higher%20life%20satisfaction.

82. Walton K, Horton NJ, Rifas-Shiman SL, et al. Exploring the Role of Family Functioning in the Association Between Frequency of Family Dinners and Dietary Intake Among Adolescents and Young Adults. JAMA Netw Open. 2018;1(7):e185217. Published 2018 Nov 2. doi:10.1001/jamanetworkopen.2018.5217

Chapter Two - Discipline

83. Jose Marti. Source: https://en.wikiquote.org/wiki/Jos%C3%A9_Mart%C3%AD

84. Koukouli S, Kalaitzaki AE. Recollections of Maternal and Paternal Punitive Discipline in Childhood and Violent Attitudes and Behaviors in Adulthood: A Mediation Model. Violence Vict. 2021;36(3):381-400. doi:10.1891/VV-D-19-00005

85. Cano-Lozano MC, León SP, Contreras L. Relationship between Punitive Discipline and Child-to-Parent Violence: The Moderating Role of the Context

and Implementation of Parenting Practices. Int J Environ Res Public Health. 2021;19(1):182. Published 2021 Dec 24. doi:10.3390/ijerph19010182

86. Sege RD, Siegel BS; COUNCIL ON CHILD ABUSE AND NEGLECT; COMMITTEE ON PSYCHOSOCIAL ASPECTS OF CHILD AND FAMILY HEALTH. Effective Discipline to Raise Healthy Children [published correction appears in Pediatrics. 2019 Feb;143(2):]. Pediatrics. 2018;142(6):e20183112. doi:10.1542/peds.2018-3112

87. Moffitt, T. E., et al. 2011. A gradient of childhood self-control predicts health, wealth, and public safety. Proceedings of the National Academy of Sciences of the U.S.A. 108:2693–2698.

88. Baumeister, R. F., and J. Tierney. 2011. Willpower: Rediscovering the Greatest Human Strength. New York: Penguin.

89. Casey, B. J., et al. 2011. Behavioral and neural correlates of delay of gratification 40 years later. Proceedings of the National Academy of Sciences of the U.S.A. 108:14998–15003.

90. Edward L. Deci and Richard M. Ryan. Intrinsic Motivation and Self-Determination in Human Behavior. University of Rochester Rochester, SPRINGER SCIENCE+BUSINESS MEDIA. LLC. New York, 1985.

91. P Nieman, S Shea, Canadian Paediatric Society, Community Paediatrics Committee, Effective discipline for children, Paediatrics & Child Health, Volume 9, Issue 1, January 2004, Pages 37–41, https://doi.org/10.1093/pch/9.1.37

92. Maccoby, E.E. and Martin, J.A. (1983) Socialization in the context of the family: Parent-child interaction. In: Hetherington, E.M., Ed., Handbook of Child Psychology: (Vol. 4.) Socialization, Personality, and Social Development, 4th Edition, Routledge, New York, 1-101.

93. Howard BJ. Discipline in early childhood. Pediatr Clin North Am. 1991;38(6):1351-1369. doi:10.1016/s0031-3955(16)38224-4

94. Positive discipline. Source: https://en.wikipedia.org/wiki/Positive_discipline

95. Source: https://www.positivediscipline.com/

96. Source: https://www.verywellfamily.com/what-is-gentle-discipline-1095046

97. Source: https://www.verywellfamily.com/what-is-gentle-parenting-5189566

98. Source: https://en.wikipedia.org/wiki/Dr._Seuss

99. Source: https://www.goodreads.com/quotes/943846-children-want-the-same-things-we-want-to-laugh-to

100. Source: https://www.verywellfamily.com/boundary-based-discipline-techniques-1095039

101. Source: https://www.verywellmind.com/what-is-authoritative-parenting-2794956

102. Fletcher, A. C. & Jefferies, B. C. (1999). Parental mediators of associations between parental authoritative

parenting and early adolescent substance use. Journal of Early Adolescence, 19(4), 465-487.

103. Christine Carter. Emotion Coaching: One of the Most Important Parenting Practices in the History of the Universe. March 19, 2009. Source: https://greatergood.berkeley.edu/article/item/emotion_coaching_one_of_the_most_important_parenting_practices_in_the_histo

104. Amy Morin. How to Use Emotion Coaching With Your Kids. Updated on February 23, 2020. Source: https://www.verywellfamily.com/emotion-coaching-discipline-process-1095040

105. Ashley Abramson. Cultivating empathy. Vol. 52 No. 8 Print version: page 44. Date created: November 1, 2021. Source: https://www.apa.org/monitor/2021/11/feature-cultivating-empathy

Chapter Three - Freedom

106. Servais Theodore Pinckaers.(1995) The Sources Of Christian Ethics. The Catholic University of America Press. Washington, D.C.

107. Robert Barron. The Glory of God is a Human Being 'Fully Alive.' January 2006. Source: https://www.wordonfire.org/articles/barron/the-glory-of-god-is-a-human-being-fully-alive/

108. Cara DiYanni. The Incredibly High Value of Free Play. Posted March 31, 2021. Source: https://www.psychologytoday.com/us/blog/play-and-imitation/202103/the-incredibly-high-value-free-play

109. Nijhof SL, Vinkers CH, van Geelen SM, et al. Healthy play, better coping: The importance of play for the development of children in health and disease. Neurosci Biobehav Rev. 2018;95:421-429. doi:10.1016/j.neubiorev.2018.09.024

110. Angela Hanscom. The Therapeutic Benefits of Free Play Outdoors. Published December 2015. Source: https://playgroundprofessionals.com/playground/nature-play/therapeutic-benefits-free-play-outdoors

111. Vincent Iannelli. The Importance of Free Play for Kids. Updated on July 02, 2021. Source: https://www.verywellfamily.com/the-importance-of-free-play-2633113.

112. Yogman M, Garner A, Hutchinson J, et al. The Power of Play: A Pediatric Role in Enhancing Development in Young Children. Pediatrics. 2018;142(3):e20182058. doi:10.1542/peds.2018-2058

113. Ginsburg KR; American Academy of Pediatrics Committee on Communications; American Academy of Pediatrics Committee on Psychosocial Aspects of Child and Family Health. The importance of play in promoting healthy child development and maintaining strong parent-child bonds. Pediatrics. 2007;119(1):182-191. doi:10.1542/peds.2006-2697

114. Amanda Rock. Benefits of Structured Play for Young Children. Updated on April 16, 2020. Source: https://www.verywellfamily.com/structured-play-2764980

115. The scientific case for learning through play. Source: https://learningthroughplay.com/explore-the-research/the-scientific-case-for-learning-through-play/

116. Benefits of physical activity. Source: https://www.canada.ca/en/public-health/services/being-active/children-physical-activity.htmlde doi:10.3945/ajcn.2010.29786

117. Onis M, Blössner M, Borghi E. Global prevalence and trends of overweight and obesity among preschool children. Am J Clin Nutr. 2010;92(5):1257-1264.

118. Task Force on Childhood Obesity. Source: https://en.wikipedia.org/wiki/Task_Force_on_Childhood_Obesity#:~:text=The%20Childhood%20Obesity%20Task%20Force,Task%20Force%20on%20Childhood%20Obesity.

119. Physical Activity Boosts Brain Health. Source: https://www.cdc.gov/nccdphp/dnpao/features/physical-activity-brain-health/index.html

120. Bidzan-Bluma I, Lipowska M. Physical Activity and Cognitive Functioning of Children: A Systematic Review. Int J Environ Res Public Health. 2018;15(4):800. Published 2018 Apr 19. doi:10.3390/ijerph15040800

121. Di Liegro CM, Schiera G, Proia P, Di Liegro I. Physical Activity and Brain Health. Genes (Basel). 2019;10(9):720. Published 2019 Sep 17. doi:10.3390/genes10090720

122. Morgan Griffin. Your Kid's Brain on Exercise. Source: https://www.webmd.com/parenting/features/kid-brain-exercise#1

123. Exploring the Use of Role-playing Games in Education. Richard Heinz, Patrick Prager. Master of Teaching Research Journal, Issue 2, 2019

124. Peter G Stromberg. Are Role-Playing Gamers Insane? Posted March 18, 2010. Source: https://www.psychologytoday.com/ca/blog/sex-drugs-and-boredom/201003/are-role-playing-gamers-insane

125. Cara Goodwin. Pandemic Parenting. Posted July 31, 2021. Source: https://www.psychologytoday.com/ca/blog/parenting-translator/202107/pandemic-parenting

126. Ecclesiastes 4:12. International Standard Version (ISV) Copyright © 1995-2014 by ISV Foundation. ALL RIGHTS RESERVED INTERNATIONALLY. Used by permission of Davidson Press, LLC. New International Reader's Version.

Chapter 4 - Instruction

127. Reiss AL, Abrams MT, et al. Brain development, gender and IQ in children: a volumetric imaging study. Brain. 1996;119(5):1763–1774. doi: 10.1093/brain/119.5.1763.

128. Stiles J, Jernigan TL. The basics of brain development. Neuropsychol Rev. 2010;20(4):327-348. doi:10.1007/s11065-010-9148-4

129. Meltzoff AN, Moore MK. Imitation of facial and manual gestures by human neonates. Science. 1977;198:75–78.

130. Meltzoff, A.N. and Moore, M.K. (1983). "Newborn Infants Imitate Adult Facial Gestures", Child Development, 54, 702-709.

131. di Pellegrino G, Fadiga L, Fogassi L, Gallese V, Rizzolatti G. Understanding motor events: a neurophysiological study. Exp Brain Res. 1992;91(1):176-180. doi:10.1007/BF00230027

132. Gallese V, Fadiga L, Fogassi L, Rizzolatti G. Action recognition in the premotor cortex. Brain. 1996;119 (Pt 2):593-609. doi:10.1093/brain/119.2.593

133. Alessandroni N. Development of Metaphorical Thought before Language: the Pragmatic Construction of Metaphors in Action. Integr Psychol Behav Sci. 2017;51(4):618-642. doi:10.1007/s12124-016-9373-3

134. Kaduk K, Bakker M, Juvrud J, et al. Semantic processing of actions at 9 months is linked to language proficiency at 9 and 18 months. J Exp Child Psychol. 2016;151:96-108. doi:10.1016/j.jecp.2016.02.003

135. Ismail FY, Fatemi A, Johnston MV. Cerebral plasticity: Windows of opportunity in the developing brain. Eur J Paediatr Neurol. 2017;21(1):23-48. doi:10.1016/j.ejpn.2016.07.007

136. Infants (0-1 year of age) Developmental Milestones. Source: https://www.cdc.gov/ncbddd/childdevelopment/positiveparenting/infants.html

137. Flavell JH, Green FL, Flavell ER, Grossman JB. The development of children's knowledge about inner speech. Child Dev. 1997;68(1):39-47.

138. Keen R. The development of problem solving in young children: a critical cognitive skill. Annu Rev Psychol. 2011;62:1-21. doi:10.1146/annurev.psych.031809.130730

139. Committee on the Science of Children Birth to Age 8: Deepening and Broadening the Foundation for Success; Board on Children, Youth, and Families; Institute of Medicine; National Research Council; Allen LR, Kelly BB, editors. Transforming the Workforce for Children Birth Through Age 8: A Unifying Foundation. Washington (DC): National Academies Press (US); 2015 Jul 23. 4, Child Development and Early Learning. Available from: https://www.ncbi.nlm.nih.gov/books/NBK310550/

140. Bargh JA. What have we been priming all these years? On the development, mechanisms, and ecology of nonconscious social behavior. Eur J Soc Psychol. 2006;36(2):147-168. doi:10.1002/ejsp.336

141. Bargh JA. Conditional automaticity: Varieties of automatic influence in social perception and cognition. In: Uleman JS, Bargh JA, editors. Unintended thought. New York: Guilford; 1989. pp. 3–51.

142. Bargh JA. Bypassing the will: Towards demystifying the nonconscious control of social behavior. In: Hassin R, Uleman J, Bargh J, editors. The new unconscious. New York: Oxford; 2005. pp. 37–58.

143. Tooley KM, Traxler MJ. Implicit learning of structure occurs in parallel with lexically-mediated syntactic priming effects in sentence comprehension. J Mem Lang. 2018;98:59-76. doi:10.1016/j.jml.2017.09.004

144. Source: https://en.wikipedia.org/wiki/Publilius_Syrus

145. Pomerantz EM, Dong W. Effects of mothers' perceptions of children's competence: the moderating role of mothers' theories of competence. Dev Psychol. 2006;42(5):950-961. doi:10.1037/0012-1649.42.5.950

146. Logan JAR, Justice LM, Yumuş M, Chaparro-Moreno LJ. When Children Are Not Read to at Home: The Million Word Gap. J Dev Behav Pediatr. 2019;40(5):383-386. doi:10.1097/DBP.0000000000000657

147. Pediatric Academic Societies Meeting. Reading with children starting in infancy gives lasting literacy boost. May 4, 2017. Source: https://bit.ly/3oBswtD

148. The Canadian Paediatric Society. POSITION STATEMENT: Read, Speak, Sing: Promoting early literacy in the health care setting. Posted: Jan 27, 2021. Source: https://cps.ca/en/documents/position/read-speak-sing-promoting-literacy

149. Diamond A. Executive functions. Annu Rev Psychol. 2013;64:135-168. doi:10.1146/annurev-psych-113011-143750

150. National Institute for Literacy. A Child Becomes a Reader. Third Edition 2006. Source: https://lincs.ed.gov/publications/pdf/reading_pre.pdf

151. Chick, N. (2013). Metacognition. Vanderbilt University Center for Teaching. Retrieved [todaysdate] from https://cft.vanderbilt.edu/guides-sub-pages/metacognition/

152. Active Listening. Source: https://www.mindtools.com/CommSkll/ActiveListening.htm

153. 9 Types of Mnemonics to Improve Your Memory. Esther Heerema, MSW Updated on June 20, 2022. Source: https://www.verywellhealth.com/memory-tip-1-keyword-mnemonics-98466

154. Reciprocal Teaching. Source: https://www.readingrockets.org/strategies/reciprocal_teaching#:~:text=Reciprocal%20teaching%20refers%20to%20an,generating%2C%20clarifying%2C%20and%20predicting.

155. Dweck, Carol S. (2000). Self-theories: their role in motivation, personality, and development. Philadelphia, PA. ISBN 1-84169-024-4. OCLC 44401375.

156. Rubin Khoddam. The Myth of Motivation. Stop searching for motivation and start taking massive action. Posted August 1, 2017. Source: https://www.psychologytoday.com/ca/blog/the-addiction-connection/201708/the-myth-motivation

157. Bible. Psalm 139:14 (ESV) "I praise you, for I am fearfully and wonderfully made. Wonderful are your works; my soul knows it very well." Source: https://biblehub.com/esv/psalms/139.htm

158. Dwayne Godwin, Jorge Cham. Your Brain by the Numbers. Scientific American. November 1, 2012. Source: https://www.scientificamerican.com/article/mind-in-pictures-your-brain-by-the-numbers/

159. Hebb, D.O. (1949). The Organization of Behavior. New York: Wiley & Sons.

160. Types of Memory (Reviewed by Psychology Today Staff). Psychology Today. Source: https://www.psychologytoday.com/us/basics/memory/types-memory

161. Kumar Mehta. A psychologist says parents of 'exceptionally resilient and successful' kids always do these 7 things: 'Yes, some are a little intense'. Published Tue, May 11 2021 Updated Tue, May 11 2021. Source: https://www.cnbc.com/2021/05/11/how-to-raise-exceptionally-smart-resilient-success-kids-according-to-psychologist.html

Chapter 5- Worldview

162. Immanuel Kant, Paul Guyer, Allen W. Wood. (1998) Critique of Pure Reason. Cambridge University Press.

163. James W. Sire. (2014) Naming the Elephant - Worldview as a Concept (2nd Second Edition). InterVarsity Press.

164. Karichrist Offersen, Hilary Davidson, Patricia Snell Herzog. (2011) Lost in Transition. The Dark Side of Emerging Adulthood. Oxford University Press, Inc.

165. The Holy Bible, English Standard Version. ESV® Text Edition: 2016. Copyright © 2001 by Crossway Bibles, a publishing ministry of Good News Publishers. (1 John 4:8, 1 John 4:16). Source: https://www.biblegateway.com/passage/?search=1%20John+4&version=ESV

166. New International Reader's Version (NIRV). Copyright © 1995, 1996, 1998, 2014 by Biblica, Inc.®. Used by permission. All rights reserved worldwide. "For God so loved the world,[a] that he gave his only Son, that whoever believes in him should not perish but have eternal life. (John 3:16)

167. Thomas Aquinas, Saint. Summa Theologica. Rights: Public Domain. URL: http://www.ccel.org/ccel/aquinas/summa.html

168. History of Hospitals. (2022) Wikipedia. Source: https://en.wikipedia.org/wiki/History_of_hospitals#cite_note-73

169. Florez, "Espana Sagrada", XIII, 539; Heusinger, "Ein Beitrag", etc. in "Janus", 1846, I.

170. Hospitals. Treatment of the history of hospitals. (2022) Source: https://www.catholic.com/encyclopedia/hospitals

171. José Martí. Source: https://en.wikiquote.org/wiki/Jos%C3%A9_Mart%C3%AD

172. James W. Byrne. The Basis of the Natural Law in Locke's Philosophy. The Catholic Lawyer. Number 1 Volume 10, Winter 1964, Number 1. Article 6. Source: https://scholarship.law.stjohns.edu/cgi/viewcontent.cgi?article=1473&context=tcl

173. Declaration of Independence: A Transcription. Source: https://www.archives.gov/founding-docs/declaration-transcript

174. The Holy Bible, English Standard Version. ESV® Text Edition: 2016. Copyright © 2001 by Crossway Bibles, a publishing ministry of Good News Publishers. 1 Corinthians 10:29 Source: https://www.biblegateway.com/passage/?search=1%20Corinthians%2010:28-30&version=ESV

175. The Holy Bible, English Standard Version. ESV® Text Edition: 2016. Copyright © 2001 by Crossway Bibles, a publishing ministry of Good News Publishers. 1 Corinthians 10:29. Romans 14:1-5. Source: https://www.biblegateway.com/passage/?search=Romans+14%3A1-5&version=ESV

176. Source: https://www.copticchurch.net/patrology/schoolofalex2/chapter12.html

177. Origen of Alexandria. Internet Encyclopedia of Philosophy. Source: https://iep.utm.edu/origen-of-alexandria/

178. Universal Declaration of Human Rights. United Nations General Assembly in Paris on 10 December 1948 (General Assembly resolution 217 A). Source: https://www.un.org/en/about-us/universal-declaration-of-human-rights#:~:text=Article%2018,%2C%20practice%2C%20worship%20and%20observance.

179. Shouting fire in a crowded theater. Wikipedia. Source: https://en.wikipedia.org/wiki/Shouting_fire_in_a_crowded_theater

180. Jennifer Marshall. Why Does Religious Freedom Matter? REPORT Religious Liberty. The Heritage Foundation. Source: https://www.heritage.org/religious-liberty/report/why-does-religious-freedom-matter

181. Encyclopedia Britannica. Source: https://www.britannica.com/

182. Civilization. Source: https://www.worldhistory.org/civilization/

183. Socratic method. Source: https://en.wikipedia.org/wiki/Socratic_method

184. Allegory of the cave. Wikipedia. Source: https://en.wikipedia.org/wiki/Allegory_of_the_cave

185. Aristotle. Wikipedia. Source: https://en.wikipedia.org/wiki/Aristotle

186. Leroi, Armand Marie (2015). The Lagoon: How Aristotle Invented Science. Bloomsbury. ISBN 978-1-4088-3622-4.

187. Pederson, Olaf (1997) The First Universities: Studium Generale and the Origins of University Education in Europe, Cambridge University Press, ISBN 9780521594318

188. Rudy, Willis (1984) The Universities of Europe, 1100-1914. Cranbury, NJ: Associated University Presses.

189. Lynn White. (1966) Medieval Technology and Social Change. Oxford University Press.

190. Jean Gimpel.(1976) The medieval machine : the industrial revolution of the Middle Ages. Publisher: Holt, Rinehart and Winston.

191. D'Souza, D.. (2007) What's So Great About Christianity. Edition: 2nd prt. Regnery Publishing.

192. Hillerbrand, Hans J.. (1968) The Protestant Reformation (Documentary History of Western Civilization). Harper Perennial.

193. List of Christians in science and technology. wikipedia. Source: https://en.wikipedia.org/wiki/List_of_Christians_in_science_and_technology

194. Source: https://en.wikipedia.org/wiki/Christianity_and_science

195. Source: List of Jewish scientists. Wikipedia. Source: https://en.wikipedia.org/wiki/List_of_Jewish_scientists

196. Polkinghorne, John. Source: https://www.questionsoftruth.org/john-polkinghorne-quotes/

197. Charles Townes. Source: https://www.azquotes.com/author/29179-Charles_Hard_Townes

198. Pew Research Center. Why America's 'nones' left religion behind. Source: https://www.pewresearch.org/fact-tank/2016/08/24/why-americas-nones-left-religion-behind/ AUGUST 24, 2016

199. Source: https://biblearchaeologyreport.com/2021/04/02/top-ten-discoveries-related-to-jesus/

200. Conca, Marco, Fanti, Giulio, Malfi, Pierandrea. (2016) The shroud of Turin : first century after Christ!. Pan Stanford Publishing

https://magiscenter.com/wp-content/uploads/2017/07/Science_and_the_Shroud_of_Turin-1.pdf

201. Spitzer, Robert J. (2015) Science and the Shroud of Turin. Magis Center of Reason and Faith. Source: https://magiscenter.com/wp-content/uploads/2017/07/Science_and_the_Shroud_of_Turin-1.pdf

202. Pirn van Lommel, Ruud van Wees, Vincent Meyers, Ingrid Elfferich. (2001) Near-death experience in survivors of cardiac arrest: a prospective study in the Netherlands. DOI: 10.1016/s0140-6736(01)07100-8

203. Ring, Kenneth, and Sharon Cooper. 1997. "Near-Death and Out-of-Body Experiences in the Blind: A Study of Apparent Eyeless Sight." Journal of Near-Death Studies, 16: 101–147.

204. Parnia, Sam, and Peter Fenwick. 2002. "Near Death Experiences in Cardiac Arrest: Visions of a Dying Brain or Visions of a New Science of Consciousness." Resuscitation, 52: 5–11.

205. Meyer, Stephen C. . DNA by Design: An Inference to the Best Explanation for the Origin of Biological Information. Rhetoric & Public Affairs, 1998, Volume:1 DOI: 10.1353/rap.2010.0105

206. Peterson To Rogan: Bible 'Precondition For The Manifestation Of Truth,' 'Way More True Than Just True'. Daily Wire News. Jan 26, 2022. Source: DailyWire.com

207. Craig, William L.. #182 Is the Cause of the Universe an Uncaused, Personal Creator of the Universe. reasonablefaith.org October 11, 2010. Source: https://www.reasonablefaith.org/writings/question-answer/is-the-cause-of-the-universe-an-uncaused-personal-creator-of-the-universe

208. Frank Pastore. Does God Exist? 4 New Arguments. Source: https://www.prageru.com/video/does-god-exist-4-new-arguments

209. Chelsea Toledo, Kirstie Saltsman. Genetics by the Numbers. National Institutes of Health. Posted June 12, 2012. Source: https://www.nigms.nih.gov/education/Inside-Life-Science/Pages/genetics-by-the-numbers.aspx

210. Gates, Bill. (1995) The Road Ahead, Penguin Group, New York, p. 188.

211. Matange K, Tuck JM, Keung AJ. DNA stability: a central design consideration for DNA data storage systems. Nat Commun. 2021;12(1):1358. Published 2021 Mar 1. doi:10.1038/s41467-021-21587-5

212. DNA Data Storage Market Size, Growth 2022 Global Industry Revenue, Business Demand and Applications (Press Release). Market Research Report to 2026

Published: April 12, 2022 at 6:33 a.m. ET Source: https://www.marketwatch.com/press-release/dna-data-storage-market-size-growth-2022-global-industry-revenue-business-demand-and-applications-market-research-report-to-2026-2022-04-12

213. J. Maddox, What Remains To Be Discovered: Mapping the Secrets of the Universe, the Origins of Life, and the Future of the Human Race, page 131 (1999 reprint, New York, NY: Touchstone, 1998

214. Wickramasinghe, Chandra. Interview in London Daily Express (August 14, 1981) Source: http://www.ideacenter.org/contentmgr/showdetails.php/id/740

215. James Tour. Scientists are Clueless on the Origin of Life. Lecture at Andrews University. Source: https://www.youtube.com/watch?v=OYHHIBIZF8o

216. Davies, Davies Paul Charles William. (1998) The Fifth Miracle: The Search for the Origin and Meaning of Life. Simon & Schuster; Allen Lane.

217. Wigner, Eugene P. (1960), "The Unreasonable Effectiveness of Mathematics in the Natural Sciences," Communications of Pure and Applied Mathematics 13: 1-14. Source: https://iep.utm.edu/math-app/

218. McGinn, Colin. (1999). The Mysterious Flame. New York: Basic Books.

219. The Holy Bible, English Standard Version. ESV® Text Edition: 2016. Copyright © 2001 by Crossway Bibles, a publishing ministry of Good News Publishers. John 1:1 Source: https://www.biblegateway.com/passage/?search=John%201&version=ESV

220. Yourdictionary. Source: https://www.yourdictionary.com/secularism

221. Physics of the Observer. Closer to Truth. (Interviews) Source: https://www.closertotruth.com/series/physics-the-observer

222. Quoted by: Norman L. Geisler, Frank Turek, David Limbaugh. (2004) I Don't Have Enough Faith to Be an Atheist. Crossway Books.

223. David Chalmers. The Hard Problem of Consciousness. (2007) The Blackwell Companion to Consciousness. Edited by Max Velmans, Susan Schneider. Blackwell Publishing Ltd.

224. James Allan Francis. One Solitary Life. "The Real Jesus and Other Sermons". Published in 1926 by Judson Press in Philadelphia (p. 123-124 "Arise Sir Knight!").

Source: http://www.spirituality.org/is/173/08.asp

225. Gary R. Habermas, The Minimal Facts Approach to the Resurrection of Jesus: The Role of Methodology as a Crucial Component in Establishing Historicity. Liberty University. STR 3/1 (Summer 2012) 15–26

226. Habermas, Gary R., and Michael R. Licona. The Case for the Resurrection of Jesus. Grand Rapids: Kregel, 2004.

227. Swinburne, Richard. The Resurrection of God Incarnate. Oxford: Oxford University Press, 2002.

228. Wright, N. T. The Resurrection of the Son of God. Christian Origins and the Question of God 3. Minneapolis: Augsburg Fortress, 2003.

229. Lee Strobel. (2016) The Case for Christ: A Journalist's Personal Investigation of the Evidence for Jesus. Zodervan, Grand Rapids, Michigan.

230. C.S. Lewis. Quote. Source: https://www.goodreads.com/quotes/26465-christianity-if-false-is-of-no-importance-and-if-true

231. G.K. Chesterton. What's Wrong with the World? Source: https://www.chesterton.org/wrong-with-world/

232. Saint Augustine of Hippo. Confessions.

233. Lewis, C. S. (2001) Weight of Glory: And Other Addresses: No. 15 (Collected Letters of C.S. Lewis). Published by Harper One.

234. José Martí. Quotes. Source: https://www.brainyquote.com/quotes/jose_marti_225374

www.ingramcontent.com/pod-product-compliance
Lightning Source LLC
Chambersburg PA
CBHW072054110526
44590CB00018B/3169